Voice in the American West

Andy Wilkinson
Series Editor

Also in the series

Cowboy's Lament: A Life on the Open Range
Frank Maynard; edited by Jim Hoy

If I Was a Highway
Michael Ventura

In My Father's House: A Memoir of Polygamy
Dorothy Allred Solomon

Llano Estacado: An Island in the Sky
Stephen Bogener and William Tydeman, editors

A Sweet Separate Intimacy: Women Writers of the American Frontier, 1800–1922
Susan Cummins Miller, editor

Texas Dance Halls: A Two-Step Circuit
Gail Folkins and J. Marcus Weekley

Rightful Place

To Tom +
Kathy

May you find our rightful place

Ang Hale Arden

Rightful Place

Amy Hale Auker

Foreword by Linda M. Hasselstrom

Texas Tech University Press

This book is typeset in Perrywood. The paper used in this book meets the mini-
mum requirements of ANSI/NISO Z39.48-1992 (R1997). ∞

Designed by Kasey McBeath

Frontispiece: *The Salt Fork in Winter*, pastel by and reprinted
courtesy of Andy Wilkinson
Map on p. xxvi: by and reprinted courtesy of Andy Wilkinson

Library of Congress Cataloging-in-Publication Data
Auker, Amy Hale, 1970–
    Rightful place / Amy Hale Auker ; foreword by Linda M. Hasselstrom.
               p. cm. — (Voice in the American West)
    Summary: "Thirty essays on land and life in the American West; poetic
prose describing the author's experiences as a wife, mother, cook, ranch hand,
and writer living the cowboy life"—Provided by publisher.
    ISBN 978-0-89672-679-6 (hardcover : alk. paper)
1. Auker, Amy Hale. 2. Authors, American—21st century—Biography. 3. Ranch
life—West (U.S.) 4. Ranch life—Poetry. I. Title.
    PS3601.U44Z46 2011
    818'.603—dc22   2010053844

Printed in the United States of America
14 15 16 17 18 19 20 21 22 / 9 8 7 6 5 4 3 2 1

ISBN 978-0-89672-887-5 (paperback) First paperback printing, 2014

Texas Tech University Press
Box 41037 | Lubbock, Texas 79409-1037 USA
800.832.4042 | ttup@ttu.edu | www.ttupress.org

To Nick Oscar Auker

Contents

Foreword

The West has received intense but sporadic attention from writers; some authorities even say there is no distinctive western literature. With *Rightful Place,* Amy Auker's voice is added to the chorus of those who prove otherwise.

> My love for the prairie crept up on me, seduced me gradually with cottonwood trees and limitless, narrative skies . . .

Western historians who have shaped our views of the West include Bernard De Voto, Frederick Jackson Turner, Wallace Stegner, Stephen Ambrose, and Howard Lamar. Lively stories of mountain men, Indians, and the fur trade, contributed by men like LeRoy R. Hafen, David Dary, "Teddy Blue" Abbott, Walter Prescott Webb, and John G. Neihardt, added variety to the western chronicles. Badger Clark popularized the rhyming cowboy, Andy Adams described his work, and Owen Wister promised he'd be dangerous but polite to women—who were mostly eastern schoolmarms. As Auker says:

> The old cowboy's sense of place is strong, though he doesn't own this short-grass country that encourages a man to love, to survive,

to know, a land that nurtures abilities unappreciated in the modern world.

Artists like Karl Bodmer, Albert Bierstadt, and George Catlin painted colorful landscapes full of flamboyant, and mostly male, characters. What symbols evoke the West? Sweeping plains? Storms and stampedes? Six-guns and spurs? Hat brims pulled low? Slow-talking gents quick on the trigger?

Many of the fable-makers, like James Fenimore Cooper, never even visited the West, but with their imitators combined mass market books, movies, and sales gimmicks into a popular vision that ignored or obliterated reality. Some westerners adopt, and promote, attractive or thrilling aspects of the western myth.

Women were always active in western life, but only a few achieved recognition as historians. Sylvia Kirk wrote of Canadian women in the fur trade, Zitkala-Sa of Lakota life, Anne M. Butler of prostitutes, Paula M. Nelson of homesteading. Mari Sandoz, ironically, celebrated her father. Willa Cather defined frontier settlements; Mary Austin explored the Southwest, and Angie Debo analyzed Oklahoma. Women like Mollie Dorsey Sanford and Elinore Pruitt Stewart recorded history in their journals. Contemporary writers like Mary Clearman Blew, Susan Armitage, Elizabeth Jameson, Terry Tempest Williams, Louise Erdrich, Linda Hogan, Teresa Jordan, Catherine Lavender, and Lillian Schlissel have filled many gaps in our history by recording and compiling the words of western women and cowgirls.

Auker says,

> Cowboys use the phrase to *sull up* when an animal or human becomes sullen and refuses to cooperate. A cow who is hot and mad will sull up and hide in the brush. . . . Ranch wives sull up, cross their arms, and raise their eyebrows for a variety of reasons.

After Patricia Nelson Limerick demonstrated how western history had been distorted and falsified by excluding women and natives, we began to learn more of the truth from writers like Denise Chavez, Maxine Hong Kingston, Susan Power, Deirdre McNamer, Amy Tan, Hisaye Yamamoto, and others.

> The women standing around me are getting quieter, but the men
> just get louder and more prophetic, profane, and profound.

Still, no one has written this story.

Amy Auker leads us into the life of the modern cowboy, his wife and children. Her family has lived on big modern ranches like the Fulton Quien Sabe, the Pitchfork, and the JA, as well as small, independently owned and operated spreads where "the boss ate lunch at our kitchen table five days a week."

> My husband changed jobs and we moved. He changed jobs and
> we moved again. And I found myself lost, having lost two babies
> in two years as my living children moved, in ever-widening circles,
> around me.

She began writing with "the old theme of no longer seeing motherhood as the epitome of female existence." Her essays weave together the work done to grow meat for Americans, and the lives of those who put it on the table. Hundreds of bovines, often steers born in Mexico, graze thousands of acres of range on huge western ranches. The owners are generally absent; hired cowboys care for the cattle. Many of these men remain single; if they are married, their wives may work for little or no pay. The family may have no health or life insurance and receive no hazard pay for this dangerous profession. In all weather, and at all hours, they ride the range to feed, nurse, fence, move, check, corral, brand, rope, guard, and finally haul to market the beef that feeds the country.

> Now my face is powdered with dirt, and my nose is red with cold.
> My eyes are burning, and my forearms ache.

If the ranch provides a house, it is often primitive and always a long, dusty distance from towns with grocery stores, doctors, schools. The contrast of ranch life with the bustle of the city is shocking to those who spend their lives on the plains.

> Every human being is going somewhere. Even the asphalt, con-
> crete, and glass scream hurry, hurry, hurry. . . . Humanity blurs on
> the streets, brand names, not people, homogeneous units of steel
> and rubber. Dodge, Ford, Subaru, Chevrolet, Toyota, Hummer.

A cowboy, often fired without notice, loses his home, takes the kids out of school, and looks for another temporary job.

> I am not allowed, in this place, to touch or capture or hold.

Auker describes the life of many modern western ranch women clearly and with painful honesty. The prairie, she says, is sometimes "bitchy," but so much a part of her that, "I don't know where I end and where the granite begins." In true western fashion she declines to whine or apologize. "Everything I do must be toward a handmade life, custom-building my days out of the fabrics of my choice." The reader may observe as she reinvents herself; she camps in remote spots, hikes through sage and bear grass, gathers cow patties for her evening fire, floats in cattle watering tanks.

> Now I can't live without the wide open sky or the cleansing wind.
> My heart knows the buffalo grass.

Searching for knowledge of herself and the land, she first explored books, poems, and songs, but eventually abandoned written words for the prairie, "laying aside my clocks, my walls, my preconceptions." She immersed herself in the country until weather became a dear friend with whom, she says, "I dance every day." And always, she wrote.

Having learned to stand toe to toe with any problem, to work beside her man, Auker retains her own individuality, the courage and strength that mark a western woman. Although she insists she is "smearing the sharp primary colors of my emotions over the land," she doesn't tell the reader how she feels. She describes her life and assumes readers are astute enough to see the anguish as well as the joys. When a young cowboy dies, for example, his friends cannot, or will not, discuss it. They talk instead of things that can be fixed. As she identifies more closely with the land and the silences it imposes on those who love it, Auker withdraws from what most folks think of as civilization:

> This seeking of and walking in tandem with the wildness and the shifting seasons robbed me of any affinity for pavement, concrete, or artificial schedules . . . caused me to . . . avoid paths with handrails.

Like many western women writers, Auker first wrote humorous first-person stories of ranch life, published in magazines and weekly newspapers. Cowboy poetry, which has garnered huge audiences in recent years, is often humorous as well; perhaps the mockery distracts western rural folks from the frustrating forces that affect our lives. But the joviality may also obscure or minimize the demanding work these men, women, and children do.

> The land has given me a love for the poetic . . . for dirt roads that snake off into the grass . . . for wounding and the healing that comes with time, for roots that make us who we are and strong enough to overcome, for a culture that both liberates and suppresses.

Auker writes, sparely but poetically, of her own wounds, and those of the western communities in which she has lived. She quotes an old Spanish proverb, "Every horseman rides beside an open grave," in an essay describing some of the grim realities: friends whose pickups don't make it around the sharp curve and who die—or worse, don't die. Horses and wild animals are killed by manmade objects that shouldn't hurt them but do; life miscarries in myriad ways. The work goes on; the prairie and its people adapt, and mostly survive.

> Two old men sit in the coffee shop. Their weather talk is laden with doom. Born into agriculture and weather, they speak the contemplative language fluently. . . . There is a storm approaching from the north, and it is never a good storm or a normal storm. It brings back memories of another storm, another time, another cold front. . . . Two old men sit in the coffee shop.

"A human being," says Amy Auker, "must live one step at a time, looking out windows and going through doors. I came to this place, my rightful place, through choice, decision, and progression."

Unless you are familiar with the lingo of the ranching west, begin by reading Auker's glossary essay, "Language of Place, Language of Work." Then you will be ready to join her on this walk, and enjoy this powerful chapter in the real literature of the West.

Linda M. Hasselstrom
Rancher, writer

#

Twenty years ago I borrowed a wedding dress and piled my long blonde hair on top of my head. I chose blue and burgundy as my colors in a decade of homes decorated with mauve southwest zigzags, bow-tied ducks, teddy bears, and Holstein cows. We stacked bales of alfalfa in front of calico-covered lattices to form an alcove in the King County community center where I had attended a formal sports banquet at the end of my senior year, 4-H meetings, baby showers, Christmas parties, and my own wedding shower. There in that alcove my sister and I stood with baby's breath in our hair while I married a South Dakota farm boy turned Pitchfork Ranch cowboy.

Nick and I drove away from our wedding reception in a blue and white Dodge pickup covered in Vaseline, shaving cream, and birdseed. We spent two nights in the honeymoon suite of the Ramada Inn in Snyder, Texas, before buying groceries and a broom and heading out to a cow camp north of Big Lake. I was nineteen years old. Nick was twenty-five. Six weeks later, armed with my new wedding present cookbooks and a recipe for green chile enchilada casserole my mother read to me over the phone, I cooked for cowboys during spring works. Over the next eighteen years we lived on cow camps on several big outfits, including the Fulton Quien Sabe, the Pitchfork, and the JA, as well as small, independently owned and operated ranches where the boss ate lunch at our kitchen table five days a week. We lived on the Quien Sabe when our son was born, and we named him Oscar after Nick's maternal grandfather. Our daughter, Lily Rose, was born four years later while we lived at Davis Camp, a JA Ranch lease, south of Clarendon, Texas.

My life as a writer was born when I wrote a letter to John Erickson, reaching out from that cow camp down in the cedar breaks to someone I hoped had an understanding of the culture and would need no apologies for the lifestyle. That first letter began, "Dear Mr. Erickson, Today I whacked a bobcat over the head with my broom." From that letter, and John's enthusiastic support, sprang a collection of humorous first-person stories of ranch life that were published in western magazines and small-town weekly newspapers. The encouragement to complete "fifty-two more just like those" fed my innate enthusiasm, the all-or-nothing facet of my personality, if not my ability to be a good writer. But even a working ranch cowboy is hard to poke fun at for too many pages—and most of the lifestyle is grotesquely un-funny from any angle.

About the time I was drifting away from the world of syndicated publishing, I met Karin Hebbert, who was living with her own working ranch cowboy and kids in the glory of the Davis Mountains in far southwest Texas. She had read one of my articles in *Western Horseman,* and stalked me through the bit and spur show at the Western Heritage Classic in Abilene with an eagerness that would flavor our friendship for years to come. We wrote voluminous letters that strained the seams of long white envelopes and made us eager to drive over rough ranch roads to the mailbox. We finally resorted to small square diskettes, saving long documents complete with clip art illustrating our observations of our simple lives: homeschooling, weather and seasons, spring and fall works, how tired were our husbands, how painful were our sorrows, how perfect were our children, how impossible it was for our mothers to understand. And, always, what we were cooking and what we were eating and what we were feeding our children and what we were planting for future meals, for what we were feeling seemed all wrapped up in how good the bread smelled as it came out of the oven.

The two of us wrote down our lives for each other in bits and spurts during busy days, in the dark quiet of the house in the middle of the night, with a steaming cup of coffee after the cowboys had left but before the children awoke—moments of passionate reflection. Though I did not know it, those long letters were honing my craft to better serve my art in the future.

My husband changed jobs and we moved. He changed jobs and we moved again. And I found myself lost, having lost two babies in two years as my living children moved, in ever-widening circles around me, away from me, a bungee cord motion of out, away, back, out, away, back, but always less back. It was the old theme of no longer seeing motherhood as the epitome of female existence, but I lacked a definition of who I was beyond nurturer and hostess, maker of bread and tortillas.

I ran to two places for solace. First, I ran to the land. And when I came back into the house with flushed face and full heart, I ran to the keyboard. I was becoming enamored with the watershed of the Salt Fork of the Red River, that place where I found myself when I needed it most. I wrote about colors, blue herons, blizzards, eggs warm in the nests, long-legged colts on yellow pastures, then splashed them indiscriminately around the world via e-mail until a kind but firm hand reined me to a stop.

I sat on a bench in the Panhandle Plains Historical Museum and listened to Andy Wilkinson talk about art, art and sense of place, living a life of art. He asked to see what I was currently writing, and over the next few weeks I sent him drivel that he barely commented on except to point out, occasionally, those few moments when my writing moved away from telling into showing. Two months later, over a bottle of red wine, he began to talk about the book. There was no book. I was spending long afternoons on the front porch reading essays by other people. There was no book. And then, all of a sudden, there was. Hidden within the rushing flow of my observations over the past few years were the seeds of the essays within this manuscript. And all of a sudden, there was a book. Much to my surprise, that book is a romance, the story of my falling in love.

I have been in love with the working ranch cowboy my whole life. As a girl, I sat beside my dad in coffee shops and feed stores, listening to livestock men cuss the weather, examine cattle prices, and make deals. I held the halter rope while he shod the remudas of large ranches as well as reset the shoes on people's family pets. I begged to go when he trotted off into desert mornings with crews of men on horseback. And I dreamed of living on a cow camp, of the kind of ranch romance that Texas rancher Tom Moorhouse talks about with his drawling, twanging long *a* sounds.

My love for the prairie crept up on me, seduced me gradually with cottonwood trees and limitless, narrative skies. In my efforts to look beyond the doors and windows, pavement and glass, structures and boundaries of modern-day living, I have taken advantage of a rural, and often isolated, life to become intimate with the land and its seasons. Now I can't live without the wide open sky or the cleansing wind. My heart knows the buffalo grass with its knobby winter hopefulness and ever-reaching runners.

This seeking of and walking in tandem with the wildness and the shifting seasons robbed me of any affinity for pavement, concrete, or artificial schedules. It caused me to avoid definitions that wrap ideas up in nice neat boxes, avoid paths with handrails and "Do Not Enter" signs, avoid people with narrowed eyes and half-smiles, avoid being so tied to an indoor life that the weather is only an acquaintance rather than a dear friend with whom I dance every day.

Writing this collection has not cured me of my love affairs in any way. I am as much a chronic as the steer who never loses his cough and hangs around in the sick pen all winter. And I didn't write it alone. Rather, I wrote it while holding hands with dirt and grass and sky and wind. The land has given me a love for the poetic, for things that ebb and flow, rise and fall, for dirt roads that snake off into the grass, for weathered men with lines on their faces, for kids who play pretend and understand danger, for wounding and the healing that comes with time, for roots that make us who we are and strong enough to overcome, for a culture that both liberates and suppresses, for animals, plants, weather, individuals, changing philosophies, and the colors that bookend each day.

Acknowledgments

This book has already taken me places, has already brought me more love than any one person can breathe in at a time. My appreciation and gratitude to the following people:

Tom Hale for teaching me to walk, to love, to see, and to think. Marilyn Hale for being the one who kept us all from sinking under the waves. Oscar Jake and Lily Rose, may you always remember the Pantagonians. Andy Wilkinson, my mirror in impatience, my touchstone for excellence. Molly Swets, my sister, my friend, and my grammar goddess. Shellie Derouen who has been there through it all and sends me tulips in midwinter. Carolyn Schnose for showing me that we create our own heaven and hell here on earth. All the folks at Texas Tech University Press for giving me a chance. Michael Jewell for friendship and e-mails and delicious debate. Karin Hebbert, John Erickson, Linda Hasselstrom, and Jody Logsdon.

Gail Steiger, for getting it, for everything.

Rightful Place

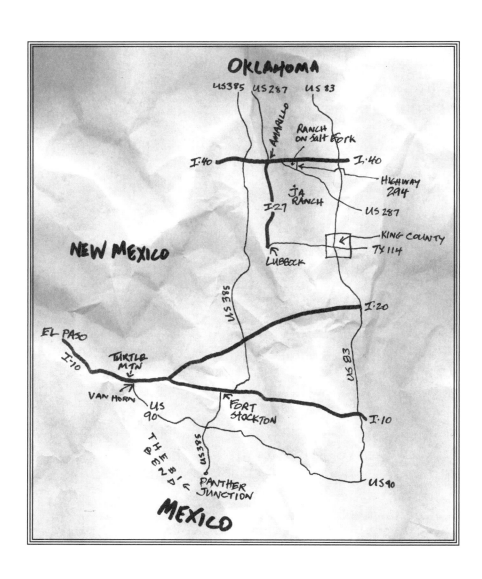

Waking Up

Turtle Mountain looms on the outskirts of Van Horn, Texas, where the school mascot is the eagle. A huge white V is painted on the turtle's shell. As a little girl, when I still thought *mightyeagles* was all one word, I would gaze at the big V from the barren playground beside the football field. My father was the senior English teacher, and each spring he took the current class of almost-graduates to refresh the whitewash on the V. I begged to go. I wanted to see the boulders piled on the mountain and smell the caustic whitewash that burned the legs of the silly girls who chose to wear shorts on the yearly outing. But it wasn't the painting of the V that attracted me as much as the opportunity to climb, to step over the desert until I could look away over the top of the town, a chance to get to know that mountain.

I never got the chance to climb Turtle Mountain. In that vast West Texas land, every mesa, every outcropping of rock, slick and tempting, every gully full of sand, every ridge of mountain with gray peaks and blue valleys called to me. I watched them flash past on Highway 54, turning in my seat to imagine myself standing on top of each highest point in succession, Guadalupe Peak looming in the north as the highest of all.

When my father left the confines of the classroom and leased a ranch north of Van Horn, I woke in the early morning hours to pull on work clothes in the dark. Long sleeves and jeans felt strange in the summertime, and my feet clomped clumsily in my boots. As we drove out of town, silence and the smell of coffee from the thermos cup filled the cab of the pickup. My favorite days were the ones when we checked or fixed fences. We rode our horses slowly, looking at each section of sagging barbed wire and at every cedar post. Even better was when we drove out to a stretch of fence and spent the whole day moving along it on foot, adding shiny stay wire and green steel t-posts to the weathered boundary lines. Daddy warned me constantly to watch for rattlesnakes and moved a bull snake from our path with a shovel while my heart thudded hard in my ears. From time to time he handed me the wet, heavy canteen, and I drank cool water that tasted of metal. In midday, we backed the pickup as far into the shade of a mesquite as we could and sat on the tailgate to eat sandwiches and fruit out of the cooler. At the end of the day, I hated pulling off my dusty boots.

———•———

On Fridays they wore short, pleated, blue and white skirts and bells on their shoes that rang through the halls as they planted their feet deliberately, hips aimed straight ahead. I knelt down on the south side of a clump of grease-wood, scraping away the caliche rocks from the ground while scraping tears from my face. I didn't want pompoms or cowbells on my shoes, but I did want to belong. My family had moved east along I-10 to Fort Stockton, where I encountered something more menacing than snakes and lechuguilla. In my old school, I had blended with the landscape. Here, as the new girl, I had found an unfavorable spotlight and a hostile social scene. I ran over and over, for the next few years, to this greasewood and caliche lot on the edge of town, its unfriendly topography more welcoming than the brand new halls of the brand new junior high.

———•———

The cemetery in King County, Texas, is a square of history, of waving grasses around crumbling monuments, of wind, of solitude, of rest. My family moved to Guthrie the summer before my senior year. I found myself captured by the romance of the old cemetery as well as by the historic ranch country along the South Wichita. Our new home was on the edge of the Town Section, a piece of land owned by the township. Rarely a day passed that I didn't walk down to the sandy river bottoms, balance my way across the cattle guard, and trudge up over the ridge until I reached the quiet grave-yard, perched on the edge of the breaks. Unbroken pastures stretched off to the north and east, the salty, sluggish river to the west and south. There, I found something I needed in the wildness that blew with the wind among the tombstones.

———•—•———

College was a groomed and manicured world where the clock ruled and my dorm room was the size of a coffin. I missed the sky. I met a starched-shirted, money-flashing, split-tongued man who bought me a gold chain. After one year in college, I went to visit him in his hometown. Three days later I drove away from him on I-20. As I drove among the sand hills east of Pecos, I looked out over the desert to the south. Then I looked east down the highway with its rules and lines and expectations. I chose the dunes. My hands turned the wheel, and the car sailed over the bar ditch, landing hard on the other side. It wiped out a barbed-wire fence, the last barrier between myself and the desert, bouncing and plowing the sand dunes until the radia-tor sucked in too much white sand. In the stillness, breathing hard, I yanked the gold chain from around my neck and fed it to the desert.

I remember little about the next several days, just worried faces, hushed voices, and questions I could not answer. I remember a bowl of cream of mushroom soup that my grandmother brought to me and how it cooled and congealed on the arm of the couch. I remember my boyfriend, freshly starched and disgusted, sitting with me for a short while. When he left, I thought that perhaps I had cried the whole time he was there, that my nose was running like a child's, and that I would never see him again. I was right on all three counts.

I had dropped the reins of my life, grabbed on to the buckboard seat and let it bounce. I remember the exact moment I reached down and picked them up again. They were harness leather split reins that fit in my left hand and smelled like a life I wanted to be a part of. It was July. My father was living on a little cow camp near Haskell, Texas, with a bedroll and a box fan. My mother, bewildered by her daughter and unwilling to stay on the camp, dumped me off and returned to her rectangular teacherage with its air-conditioning and fresh sheets.

I don't know how many days Dad and I went without speaking after his welcoming hug and "Hi, Twinkie," but I remember spending the long evenings roping the roping dummy on the front porch, and I remember the moment that he broke the silence. We were riding south at dawn.

"I know where you are. It's like being in a dark tunnel, and you think you will never see light again. I held a gun in my hand when I was in that tunnel . . . more than once. I promise you, promise you, that you will see light soon, and that it will be worth riding towards."

In that moment I became aware of the reins in my hand and the fact that the whole world had turned pink around me. I felt the regular rhythm of Bum, the kindest stud horse in the world, and the slick seat of my grandfather's old saddle beneath my thighs. That afternoon, we drove into Haskell to the Dairy Queen, seeking some relief from the triple-digit heat. The blast of cold air that hit me as we walked into the restaurant woke me up. I told my father everything.

He told me never to leave the land.

Six months later, with my father's blessing, I married a working ranch cowboy. We moved onto a remote camp where I discovered ranch roads and the fact that it doesn't take long to keep house for two. I walked for miles over caliche, sand, and the rich red dirt of the river breaks. I discovered sunsets and sunrises, cottonwood trees and animal tracks, the freedom to sing or yell at the top of my lungs, tempting cattle trails, and how much cold or wind or heat or rain I could endure. I have been walking ranch roads ever since.

Highway 294

I drive in the land of cowboys in pickups. Hat and mustache make each profile distinct. As we pass on the two-lane, each rig tells a story of the day's work and last year's markets. The make and the model, the dog and the horse, speak of the man and his work. The story of each region is told on its roads, each farm-to-market a page in its book. If the highways take us away, the little back roads take us home, and they are peopled by those who belong.

Crossing the railroad tracks, I meet an old blue Dodge sowing empty brown cake sacks behind. The grizzled driver, whose hat sports only a faint sweat mark, will park at the Dairy Queen soon. He'll pass the heat of the day drinking tea over crushed ice while a thin horse, bridled in dry leather and bits of orange twine, stomps a patient rhythm on the trailer's rotten boards. His cows are always out, his fences tied up with pieces of rusted baling wire, and his water gaps clogged with tumbleweeds. His branding pen is patched with wooden pallets and discarded bedsprings. He has a hard time finding help. No one wants to work for twenty-year-old wages, especially when dinnertime means a roll of bologna, a loaf of white bread, and a five-pound bag of ginger snaps thrown onto the tailgate.

A shiny new rig with dually tires blows by, smelling of banker's benevolence. The driver is a trust-fund youth with a cell phone instead of a mustache. He rodeos on the weekends. His hat is new, and his cows are fat. His horses are expensive and slick. He might not be ranching long, but he sure makes it look good. The weekend ropings might start paying off, or he might find a new breed of cattle and strike it richer. I see from the highway that he's put in a circle, improving his land with center-pivot irrigating and spraying. I lift my fingers in a country wave, but he hasn't gotten to know his neighbors yet.

Farther from town, I swing around the curve and wave to a cowboy in an older-model ranch truck with a well-known brand painted on the side. In the bumper-pull trailer, a saddled bay horse dries in the wind, glistening sweat turning to crusty white salt. A few miles from here, the ranch hand will pull up to the barn, strip his saddle, and turn the horse out to roll and graze. He'll spend the afternoon checking windmills and putting out the mineral blocks stacked on the flatbed of his truck. He'd rather be riding than driving, but he looks after a lot of country and is spread pretty thin. Like the Navajo blanket under his saddle, his black felt hat is sweated through. He has a new one hanging on the hat rack by the front door. This outfit pays pretty good. The ones who write his paycheck don't understand that he prowls their cattle and stops to fix every gap, that he takes pride in his camp, pride in his day, and pride in tending their brand. He'll gentle their horses, and take their money, and live on their land with his dreams.

Up ahead, I spot a pickup perpendicular to the road, and a man opening the wire gate leading into the pasture on the right. The elderly collie in the bed of the truck waves her tail as she lifts her nose to the wind. She used to be a familiar sight, as was the stooped old man she rode with. For a moment I think they are together again, but the figure climbing in the driver's side is much too spry. As he pulls through the gap in the fence, I realize that the collie is traveling with the grandson now. I hope his hands are kind, taking the time to give her elderly joints a lift. Perhaps he learned his lessons of heritage and land early, while the wise voice was still teaching. The pickup pulls off into the pasture as I pass the ghost of an old man who won't lift his hand in greeting on this stretch of road anymore.

I'm almost to my own entrance when a day worker flies by me, two horses in tow. He's always headed somewhere. He makes sixty-five dollars a day, so he's got to take up the slack by shoeing town folks' horses and bucking bales of hay in the cool. He is feeding his family and paying the rent, but a blown tire blows the day's take. He's got to scramble. He's got to ride other men's horses for pay. He'll sit and blow when the kids are raised, or he'll buckle and take a steady job. For now, he goes by so fast I don't have time to wave, but I wish him luck and dollars.

The story of the seasons is written on these back roads. On a chill spring morning, a string of working men's rigs with horses all saddled to ride bends at a rancher's gate for the first branding of the year. At noon they'll be lined up neat at the café or at some cow camp off the road. The day workers and neighbors are happy to help, though their own work awaits them at home. In autumn, noise of the big rigs, cattle pots headed for pens, shatters the morning as they swoop over hills and rumble down lanes making dust. In the afternoon, they growl back out, in intervals, heavy-laden, turning toward feedlots and sale barns. Headlights herald a tired echo some hours later as cowboys head home in the too-early dusk, the long shipping stretch at an end.

As we bump across our own cattle guard onto the dirt road, my son's monologue about pickups intrudes on my thoughts. He wants one of his own. He talks of which model will suit his purposes, as if he knows. I refer him to his father when he asks questions about gas mileage, cost, and pulling capacity, because I don't know. Someday soon, he'll turn his wheels away from this home and head for places he must go on his own. I'll wave good-bye as he heads out in the evening to pick up a date or meet a friend for some fun. One distant day, he'll roll his bed, jump a horse in the trailer, and leave our little road, looking for work and for love. He'll drive away, a cowboy in a pickup, and people who pass him will recognize the peach fuzz and bravado crease, and lift a hand in greeting.

Weather Talk

Two old men sit in the coffee shop. The ceiling fan whips in circles, splashing the warm air 'round and 'round. The two old men wear John Deere caps, or seed company caps, or fertilizer caps, or chemical company caps. The coffee is just a prop as they talk of the weather. It is too hot, and it is never going to rain again. Or perhaps it has rained too much, and their fields are boggy and glistening with standing water. Perhaps they drove out alone in the early morning to sit silently, viewing a crop flattened by hail that pounded on the roof the night before. Now they talk and sip.

Two old men sit in the coffee shop. The vent above the counter blows hot air into the busy room, already warmed by the grill where eggs and sausage sizzle. Conversation about the weather rises from the old men as steam rises from their enamel mugs. It has been a hard winter, or a mild winter, or a dry winter. There is a storm approaching from the north, and it is never a good storm or a normal storm. It brings back memories of another storm, another time, another cold front, and yet always the same pattern.

Two old men sit in the coffee shop. Their weather talk is laden with doom. Born into agriculture and weather, they speak the contemplative language fluently. Every conversation begins and ends with the weather. "Sure is a hot one, ain't it?" turns into "Well, go ahead and let it rain." They are experts with the remote control, intimate with the forecasters. They will die in agriculture and be buried in the weather, never removed from the land, from the seasons, or from the doom.

Many of their offspring and grandchildren will never speak the weather talk. For them, weather is rain pelting outside of their climate-controlled cubicles or ruining their weekend at the lake, hail putting dents in their shiny cars, and heat bleaching their small handkerchiefs of bermuda when the city restricts water usage. They will never gaze across fields already seeded, receiving the blessing of a nitrogen-laden snow in late April.

The children will drive out to the old home place and try to persuade the old man and his soft, crumpled counterpart to buy a newer car or renovate the old-fashioned house. The old man will stand, drinking coffee, staring out of a kitchen window and estimate, in his mind, the yield or the damage or the time until he can get into his fields, while their voices rise and fall in supplication for him to change his ways. His grandchildren, confiscating the remote control, will never understand why he works when it is hot or cold or windy or wet. On his next trip to the city to visit his son, he takes a rain gauge, one that his small-town bank still gives away along with tally books and pocket pens, and mounts it on the picket fence where it will quickly fill up with drowned wasps and bits of dead leaf. The children of the old men don't measure rainfall by hundredths of an inch.

The old men were my grandfather and my father, though they wore stained felt hats rather than gimme caps and measured harvests by calf crops and weaning weights rather than by bushel or bale. They were my husband's grandfathers, removed from Texas by three states, but weathering the storm and haying the meadows above the badlands of South Dakota. Perhaps, someday, my son will be one of them, living his life in the sway of nature's moods.

I alter my routine as the season for stew and cornbread, hot tea and heavy chore coat, passes into a muddy spring, and finally the gasping blister of our first hundred-degree day. My chores shift from carrying warm water to the chicken pen and pouring out Layena pellets to watering and weeding the garden. Rather than sitting at the keyboard in the bitter early morning, leaving my outdoor chores for the warmest time of day, sunrise finds me, coffee cup in one hand, green hose in the other, watering the garden while the world wakes up and before the sun drives me indoors for sweet tea with lemon, foods that can be prepared without heating up the kitchen, and writing in the heat of the day. Rather than doing barn chores in the middle of the afternoon, coming into the warm house stomping cold feet in the waning light, we stay out of doors until after suppertime, sitting in the evening breeze at the saddle house or on the porch in the lengthening days. My mudroom floor reflects the surface moisture around the camp, and the hooks on the wall reflect the temperature by the number and type of coats they support. The men eat less in the heat, but consume gallons of iced tea out of sweating mason jars. In the cold, they put away carbohydrates and coffee, insulation from the biting wind. My children celebrate the first hot day by jumping in the horse trough long before the clear water of the swimming pool in town is available. Lily helps me dig the garden on spring mornings that start off frigid but end up warm enough for us to shuck our jackets and hang them on the fence. We learn to read the wind and detect the burnt hint of fall as it blows across the prairie.

My husband works in the hot and the cold and the wind and the wet. When he meets the old men in the tire shop or at the feed store, he can tell them how much rain we got last night, not only here at the house, but in the gauge between the Dockins section and the Bull Pasture and down on the field at Red House. He asks their advice when the frost turns the wheat to poison, and he loses four head in one night to bloat. The old men shake their heads and tell him to put dishwashing liquid in the water trough or offer other home remedies and memories of other years when bloat was a problem. With them, he talks numbers and trends and forecasts as he fills his water trailer by poking quarters into the city water pump because the wind is not blowing for the x-th day in a row, the windmills are standing idle, and the steers are bawling with thirst.

In the late evening, we sit on the front porch, my husband, a neighbor friend, and I. The men tilt their hats back and pop open cold beers and talk of wet springs, chances of rain, heat waves, and how fat the cattle will be come shippin'. As they talk, I wonder if I planted too many squash vines and spot the first hummingbird about the time he spots the feeder swaying in the breeze.

The Giver

His hip hurts when he is stressed. He cried when his mother told him she had breast cancer. He's been intensely disappointed when father figures in his life have let him down. I've seen him get bucked off only twice in the last sixteen years. He pulls weeds around the perimeter of my garden on summer evenings while I water the tomatoes. Every morning he pours my coffee and doctors it with french vanilla creamer; every night he fixes the coffeepot so that he can push the button at 5:00 a.m. He reads most of the books I suggest, and drinks a lot of beer. He buys wine when he checks his cattle pastured north of Pampa, and we drink it on the front porch as the sun goes down. Sometimes he comes in from town with a Dr. Pepper over ice, just for me. His hearing is damaged from growing up in a milking barn in South Dakota, and he loves to buy sunglasses. I wonder why he thinks I am beautiful when he orders flashy boots, silver-mounted gear, and a new saddle too often. He's losing the hair on the top of his head. His hands are thick and blunt-fingered, powerful. To others, Nick is bigger than life. To me, he is the fabric of my life.

He inherited his mother's skin tone, her ability to laugh, a spirituality that goes beyond religious convictions, and her penchant for giving good gifts. He knows when it is appropriate to give me cast iron skillets for Christmas and when to surprise me with a bottle of bath oil for no reason at all. On my dresser is a poem that he found in *Reader's Digest* one summer. He saved it until Christmas and had a friend type it on white paper. He framed it in a dime-store frame, matted with construction paper from the kids' craft supplies. On Christmas Eve, he went to the florist and bought a rosebud to accompany the gift. He hid the rose in the saddle house to be retrieved when he checked the pregnant heifers before dawn the next morning. The fragile bud froze during the night. He was disappointed with the droopy presentation, but there in the lights of the Christmas tree I opened up the cheap frame, and put that poor brown rose under the glass with the poem.

He loves things that glitter and sparkle and shine and can't understand why I think gold and silver and diamonds are a hassle and stressful and unnecessary. When we got engaged, he couldn't afford to buy me a diamond ring. He was living in the bunkhouse on the Pitchfork Ranch near Guthrie, Texas, so we drove to Lubbock to the mall to shop for wedding rings. We had already decided to buy a refrigerator and a stove instead of a diamond solitaire and to opt for simple wedding bands for the ceremony. He carried his cashed paycheck in a wad in his pocket. Just as we reached Lubbock, his pickup broke down, and he had to peel off some of the bills to buy a new fuel filter. With this mechanical and financial glitch to start off the day, we walked among the shops in a daze, not knowing how to begin. Bob Moorhouse, the Pitchfork Ranch manager, and his wife, Linda, who happened to be in the mall as well that day, had just spun a promotional wheel in front of a jewelry store and won half off any purchase. When they heard why we were in town, they gave us that coupon. As I watched the wad of bills shrink to nearly nothing to pay for those simple gold bands, and as I realized how much work they represented, I struggled to hold back tears. While the rings were being sized, Nick sent me down the mall to a restaurant and told me to wait for him. He showed back up with a rose and a card that read "Just Because."

If he can't get to town during calving season to buy a Hallmark Valentine, he cuts hearts out of construction paper and scatters them around the house: one in my journal, one under my coffee cup, one on my keyboard, one wrapped around my toothbrush. I grew up without Christmas in my parents' home, so I was determined, that first year we were married, to have Christmas in a big way. Nick and I cut a cedar tree in the Croton River breaks. It filled up one whole end of our narrow living room, and we only had enough ornaments for the side that showed. Together we decorated that first tree and each one since, Nick taking over the stringing of the popcorn while I manage the production of the cranberry garland. The only problem, that first year, was that when we got all of the glass balls and painted wooden ornaments hung on the tree, we realized that I had forgotten to buy a star for the top. Nick sat down with his pocket knife and built one out of a beer box and a roll of tinfoil. Though it has been refurbished with new foil from time to time, that beer-box star is still the last thing to go on our tree each year.

With my Christmas-less background and his young adulthood spent in bunkhouses, an awkward guest at other families' celebrations, we were free to draw our own path on the clean slate of our married lives. I made him a stocking out of denim to hang beside the one my sister stitched for me, and that first year we became Santa Claus to each other. Every year we spend two months searching for just the right items to put in those stockings, items to demonstrate that we think of each other during a very busy season. Christmas Eve, when our other Santa duties are done, we sneak around, admonishing each other not to look, and using blankets to cover up what won't fit into the socks. One very cold, very dark Christmas morning, while we sat at the kitchen table waiting for our young children to wake up, we drank a whole pot of coffee and ate an entire pumpkin pie with spoons.

Spring was very wet this year, and the summer is turning into a wet summer. Because the prairie grasses have grown up tall enough to obscure the pasture roads and their tops brush my thighs, I have nowhere to walk except the caliche driveway unless I am brave enough to risk stepping on a rattlesnake in the tall grass. Last week, in the middle of the morning, in the middle of a workweek, I heard the sound of a tractor. Nick had hooked onto the shredder and was making a path up the center of the pasture road that runs north of the house. When he reached the north fence of the horse pasture he turned along it to the east, mowing a path all the way to the far fence where he turned south until he met the driveway that runs east and west. I imagine that from the air it looks like aliens have drawn a big, sloppy, wavy rectangle in the wildflowers and grama grasses. In the cool, early mornings when I walk along the mown path and the dew soaks through my shoes, I know that once again, the man who gives great gifts has done it again.

This spring he gave me the gift of ten days away from the ranch, away from being wife and mother, ten days to find my footing in my art. It was a great gift, a much-needed gift, and a gift that has been harder for me to accept than any other. Regardless of all I have learned about the gift economy of art, I still struggle with the humility that each new gift brings, knowing that I have no obligation to the giver other than to complete that gift, to fulfill its potential, husbanding it and developing it in order to give it away again. The path has been mown across the prairie, but I must walk it alone.

The Pantagonians

The ropes hanging from the rafters of the hay shed sway with the wind. The hay was unloaded into two huge stacks, perfect for neighboring castles or fortresses. The bottom layers are neat and orderly, while the top layers have been rearranged into turrets, windows, galleys, armories piled with dried gourds, sleeping platforms, and secret passageways. A friendly dragon lives in a hay bale cave. Handkerchief flags fly from cedar stays, and an Archie comic book is tucked between two bales. Treasures harvested from the old dump south of the house line the rafters of the shed, waiting to be stolen by bandits who swing across from the neighboring fortress or scale the walls in spite of a thrown-gourd defense. A bucket on a rope waits to be lowered by the gatekeeper for an afternoon snack or coded message from the laird of the next keep. A cache of weapons lies at the base of a ragged stairway: spears with rudely carved handles, knives made from scrap metal and bits of wood, sucker-rod javelins, daggers, quarterstaves, swords, dirks, a mesquite-limb bow strung with orange baling twine, a lady-sized lance. An evil pike fish lurks in the nearest moat, ready to be released into the stream should enemies approach.

Today the pike swims lazily in circles, for no defense of the abbey is needed. No warrior princess swings out over the empty spaces or treads the high castle walls. The gourds are at rest in the stockpile. The pages of the comic book flutter in the wind, and the weapons look like a pile of junk.

———•————•———

Two ships toss on the yellow prairie. The brother ship and the sister ship are anchored end to end, clippers under full sail on an arid ocean. Mature monkey people, known as squeegies, make up the ships' crews. They are good sailors because they are agile enough not to fall from the mast when keeping lookout. The younger squeegies must stay locked in cages because they are destructive and would wreak havoc with the ships as they sail. When the captains prey upon enemy vessels, the baby squeegies are allowed out of their cages to collect the loot. A troll named Grul lives on the brother ship. The ships' passengers are women warriors called Pantagonians whom the brave captains have rescued from the evil king of Spain. The captain of the brother ship also stole some of the king's cigars, an offense the king cannot forgive. The swords and daggers from the pile at the hay barn have slain many pirates in defense of the invisible gold deep in the holds. At nine years old, the sister captain excels at the fancy footwork of swordplay, while the brother captain favors a poisoned throwing star as his weapon of choice. The biggest danger on this windblown sea is a sea monster that can't be bested because his scales are made of metal. Once, the brother and sister captains captured the queen of England. They consider this one of their least finest moments because the queen kept giving the sailors refined manners lessons. The sailors were completely incapacitated because they were practicing good posture while trying to defend the ship. Meanwhile, the Pantagonians, who are somewhat like dryads but meaner, just sit around playing dice and drinking martinis.

Today, no swordfights are being won or lost atop the old boxcars where we store cow cake and mineral blocks. They are devoid of squeegies, sea battles, or captains. No sea monster thrashes in the water. The Pantagonians have put away their dice, and the king of Spain's cigars are safe.

———•————•———

The horse pasture is silent. There are no bunkhouse boys roping wild mavericks and breaking rough broncs for a living. They haven't come slamming into my kitchen to clean me out of homemade tortillas and apples to stock the larder of the plyboard bunkhouse down in the creek. I won't have to pick cactus spines out of grubby hands, worry about rattlesnakes, or exclaim over every perfect rock they found while building their ranch. Tom or Jim or Jack or Joe will not roll down a rocky slope while gathering mustangs from the wilderness. The Indian princess (who sometimes shows up when being Tom or Jim or Jack or Joe loses its appeal) won't bring me a wilted bouquet of wild flowers today. The wild plum thicket sale barn is silent, empty of auctioneer or livestock. Tom or Jim or Jack or Joe won't have his usual falling out with the boss, necessitating that he run away with the boss's daughter and establish his own ranch in the south. And the old man who lives in the dugout in the creek bank won't get his usual supply of imaginary whiskey in return for a great yarn and some shelter around his fire.

———•—•———

The back door of the Suburban opens, and four books spill out onto the driveway. Lily jumps out and kneels in the dirt while telling me the titles of the most wonderful books in the world, all of which she is trying to carry in her overfull cloth bag. I thank the other mother for taking her to the library, shake sand and rocks out of the books, and sweep the long blonde strands of hair out of my daughter's eyes. Her shoes are untied, and there is something spilled on the front of her shirt. My friend's Suburban pauses to let my husband's pickup and trailer pass before going on down the lane to the highway.

Nick and Oscar jump their horses out of the trailer. My thirteen-year-old son is impatient with his mount, and his feet drag as he walks to the barn. He listens silently as Lily chatters on and on about the newest Redwall book and how she checked out the dragon books again in case he wants to borrow them. He is taller than I am now, and his voice is deep. He lugs his saddle and saddle pad to the rack and unbridles the sweaty three-year-old who walks immediately to the water trough to drink before wandering out the open gate to roll in the sand. Oscar says, "No, Lily" when she asks if he wants to go play on the hay.

Sunset is still an hour away. The barn chores are done, but it isn't time for supper. Oscar leans against the wall as he uses the bootjack to pull off his boots and then walks slowly to his room. As I slice potatoes, I can see Lily through the window, silhouetted against the lowering sun, swinging slowly back and forth on a rope, pushing off from the hay stack over and over again. The hot grease sizzles with each fresh handful of raw potato. Oscar emerges from his room. He grabs a fry from the stack at my elbow, asks what's for supper, and grins at me as he puts on his sneakers. The back door slams.

The Pantagonians stir their martinis. The wild mustangs lift their heads in fright. The friendly dragon roars with joy. And the lonely warrior princess climbs the rope into her castle, gourds at ready to defend her lands against all comers.

Facing North

From the south side of the squeeze chute I glance at the hovering blue norther, a dark, heavy line that the wind has pushed our way all morning long. The head gate slams shut on yet another steer as he attempts to leap through the keyhole to freedom. I squeeze the triggers on the airplane-shaped vaccine guns, one shot in the neck, one in the hip. On the opposite side of the chute, Nick plants the glowing branding iron firmly against the damp curly hair of the steer's hip. The icy wind, already mixed with grit whipped up from beneath the hooves of two hundred Mexican steers, does not allow the smoke to billow upwards, but shoots it straight across the steer's back and into my watering eyes. Again.

The constant roar of the propane burner blowing blue heat onto the irons, the incessant bawling of the tired animals, the clang and bang of the head gate, and the smell of cold mixed with heat fills the air. The kids are doing their jobs like robots. Oscar keeps the snake—the narrow alley leading to the chute—full of steers, swinging his stick, manning the heavy gates, pushing, prodding, poking, persuading. Lily slides her gate open and shut, banging on the metal pipes of the snake with a stick, sweet-talking the steers along. My hands are cramped and chapped. Periodically I stop to change needles, yanking the dull one off with a pair of pliers, dropping it into the trash barrel, carefully uncapping and fitting on a new sharp one.

The day began last night. The house was getting dimmer with each light I turned off as I went around adjusting the thermostat, shutting down the computer, hugging toothpaste-scented kids good night, and filling my water glass. Nick was in the shower when the phone rang. A truckload of cattle, loaded at the Mexican border at sundown, would be here before dawn. He stood dripping, a towel around his waist, phone to his ear, and turned down the offer of a processing crew that couldn't show up until the day after. He'd rather get us to help him process the fresh cattle than let the road-weary animals stand in the pens for twenty-four hours, breathing dust. I turned the kitchen light back on and put a roast in the slow cooker, the dial set on low.

Now my face is powdered with dirt, and my nose is red with cold. My eyes are burning, and my forearms ache. Nick pulled several sick cattle out of the pasture this morning, so before we began processing the new load we ran the ones with hanging heads, drooping ears, and snotty noses through the chute for a dose of medicine. Thick yellow goo ran down my arm as repeated penetrations with a needle wallowed a hole in the gray rubber stopper of the antibiotic bottle.

Gradually, one note in the constant symphony of chaos begins to die out. The steers' bawling diminishes as more and more of them are released from the chute into a pen with hay, cow cake, and water. They are beginning to bed down. I look up to see Oscar slam the gate at the end of the snake behind the last steer to be processed. He leans his head against the rail to blink his eyes slowly, trying to wash the dirt out of his contact lenses. He is still limping from being kicked in the ankle in the crush of the sorting pen. As the last steer leaps for freedom and is trapped in the squeeze chute, Lily closes her swinging gate. I squeeze the triggers of the vaccine guns as once again a stream of branding smoke blows over me. Nick twists the valve on the propane bottle and abruptly the roar of the burner ceases. My ears ring in the relative silence as the steer leaps to freedom and joins the tired herd. I begin throwing empty medicine bottles in the barrel and dropping unused needles into the small cooler at my feet. Nick and Oscar discuss the most efficient manner of loading the steers that must be hauled to another division of the ranch while Lily and I wash our hands in the water trough and dry them on our nasty jeans. Nick keeps glancing north.

We begin shucking layers as the heater blows hot air into the pickup. Nick makes fun of Lily and me for not being real cowboys when we wash our faces with baby wipes. We borrow his ChapStick, ignoring the bits of dirt and snuff stuck to its surface. My hair smells strongly of smoke. The trip north is quiet after I open our lunch sack and pass out still-warm tortillas filled with roast beef and cheese and wrapped in tinfoil; green, crisp apples; crumbly squares of chocolate cake. The cattle are restless in the trailer, making it sway and walk all over the road.

The storm clouds sit heavy on the land, and bits of ice begin hitting the windshield as soon as we reach the pens where one of the other cowboys is waiting to help us unload. The cattle leave the trailer in a rush, and we head back to the south, not pausing to visit. The kids bury their noses in books, and the wind pushes us hard from behind. Nick grins at me as he leans over to pick a bit of dried cow manure out of my hair.

Merchandise

The stoplight barring my way onto Georgia Street glows a stubborn red. The city is in constant motion with cars and vans and pickups and trucks speeding by or waiting or turning the corner or baking in the sun. Every human being is going somewhere. Even the asphalt, concrete, and glass scream hurry, hurry, hurry. My muscles tense, and my blood revs in my veins in anticipation of my turn to move on green. Humanity blurs on the streets, brand names, not people, homogeneous units of steel and rubber, Dodge, Ford, Subaru, Chevrolet, Toyota, Hummer.

All day long I walk among choices, inanimate objects with numerical values and garish tactics to draw my hand to their packaging rather than to that of their neighbors'. All day long I make choices: made in China or the USA, sweetened or un, five pounds or ten, paper or plastic, cash or check, name brand or store knockoff, latest-and-greatest or tried-and-true. Human faces pass by in their own careful three-foot circles while the brand names seem like friends: Yoplait, Del Monte, Tide, Nestlé, Shurfine, and Folgers.

The human voice is drowned, unnoticed and unheeded. The hum of a thousand motors fills the air, powering machines that heat, cool, drive, clean, pump, and spit coins into silver trays. Doors slam or swish. Warning sounds become common enough to be ignored, honking, blaring, and whining above the rumbles of everyday life. I cannot hear the human voice singing, but within each sealed unit on the street cold air blows from vents and music blares from speakers. Interspersed among the songs are pleas from the pick-me profession, calling for us to stay and sample, urging us to carry away more than we need.

I arrive home exhausted, drained, and depleted, laden with merchandise. I lug it, bag by bag, into the house to disperse it into our lives and drawers and kitchen cabinets.

———•—•—

The water in the tub is calm and still and green. The tub, bisected by a pipe fence, waters the corrals as well as the pasture where I am keeping a group of horses that I hope to sell. I stand on the fence, leaning over the top rail, and stare downward. The goldfish that live in the depths ripple the surface when they rise to mouth the air. Their numbers ebb and flow with the appetites of the coons, owls, and blue herons. The intense pumpkin-orange fish are the most noticeable, but I stare into the algae-filled water long enough to realize that some of the others are brown, or white with orange spots, or a fine translucent gold, like the one with the chocolate brown fedora falling over his eyes. My breathing slows as they hang silently in the water or swim lazily to nowhere.

A fastidious parson walks daintily among the grasses, high-stepping in slow motion on long, angled legs. He is silent now, but I have heard his kill-dee sermon before. A ground squirrel that has been hiding in the shade since I walked up grabs this moment to dart into the weeds and disappear, a dust-colored flip of motion that pulls his entrance in after him. A meadowlark swings on the fragile stem of a mesquite bush. Over by a small puddle, a cheeky swallow gathers mud for her home. She ignores my presence with all but the very edge of her black eyes.

The horses stand on cocked hips beside the tub and switch at flies. I know the story behind each of their names. Fangs has a wicked white configuration in the middle of his forehead that reminds me of a snake. I hope when someone begins training Blue and Badger, they will earn names more indicative of their personalities rather than their coloring or breeding. Rosita is a lovely little strawberry roan with a feisty Latin temper. Sadie's eyes are those of a dance-hall girl, tired at the end of the night. Smoke is the color of his name and doesn't like to be separated from the other horses. Tell has an arrow-shaped mark on his side, and Big Enough would be the perfect sidekick in a Will James book.

Smoke sniffs the toe of my shoe before he drinks, large gulps of water making tracks up his neck. These horses have price tags. They are merchandise without fancy packaging, although Fangs carries quite a bit of color and would have caught the eye of a true plainsman. The gold in the water at my feet disappears as the fish sink to the bottom in response to a shadow trailing along the ground. I shade my eyes just in time to see a Mexican eagle disappear into a grove of trees to the north. It is only a few seconds before the fish surface again, arrogant in their ability to dive for the depths, their marble eyes quick to see the dangerous shadows before I do. Tell swishes his nose in the water in a big noisy splash. One cool drop lands on my ankle.

Badger and Blue stand as far away as is necessary to keep me from touching them. I hear more birds than I see, and their songs mingle with those of the crickets, locusts, and bees that I would have to hunt for long and hard. If I put my hand into the water, every goldfish would vanish. I am not allowed, in this place, to touch or capture or hold. If I rest here long enough, I might see the snake that made the wide undulating mark in the sand at the base of the tub, but it is more likely that I will see only the horse hoof or feel the wind that will erase it. The accessibility of this place is in my resting, my patience, my not-doing.

The door latch on the pickup is hot under my hand as I turn and look back. The horses have moved away from the water, tearing off mouthfuls of grass, walking slowly in no direction. The fish with the brown fedora must be napping in the mud at the bottom of the tub. There are no eagles flying now, no ground squirrels, and even the meadowlark has flown.

Bread Bowl

My house is full of things. Most of them are diminished with use, spoiled with time, plundered with each turn of the page, have function without appeal or appeal without function. The antique pottery bread bowl sitting on my kitchen counter holds its separateness from those other things in its utilitarian but graceful shape. It is the color of the prairie in August when the grasses have been cured and bleached by the sun. Its sides are sloped and generous, its bottom smooth and worn. The pottery is heavy and thick. My fingers are intimate with the one chip in its interior finish. It has no moving parts, no flashing lights, no intriguing sounds to alert me when the rising is done. For days on end the pottery stands empty, and yet, its bounty is inexhaustible. It acts without effort and nourishes without demanding.

The bowl was a gift from my mother-in-law, a tall, broad-shouldered woman with old hands who gives good gifts. Her skin is weathered from working in the sun and winters of South Dakota. A surgeon took her breasts but diminished her not at all. I call her Carolyn rather than Mom, but that's not how I feel.

She moves around her kitchen slowly as she cooks for large groups of people: grandchildren, cowboy crews, friends, team ropers come to play. She never hurries and rarely follows a recipe exactly as it is written. She puts the salted peanut chews under the broiler and forgets them until the marshmallows catch on fire. She makes bread with practiced motions and sets it to rise in heavy pottery bowls, never modern molded plastic or shiny stainless steel.

One summer, when she was visiting from South Dakota, we drove up out of the mesquites and cedars of the JA Ranch to prowl the dim interior of the antique store in Clarendon. When I saw the heavy bowl, I lifted its cool weight, leaving a blank circle in the dust on the shelf. After I read the faded price tag, written in pencil on masking tape curled and brittle with age, I wiped my hands on my jeans and moved on.

Later that day, Carolyn handed me a gift wrapped in a brown paper grocery sack. I knew by its weight that she had bought the bowl for me. The masking tape price tag was gone.

———+—•—+———

I grew up eating brown-and-serve rolls out of twist-tied plastic bags, crescent rolls out of thump-open cardboard tubes, and biscuits out of a yellow-boxed mix. Now I dig through Carolyn's eclectic and messy recipe collection regularly. I sort through brittle newspaper clippings and faded recipe cards written in the various hands of the women whose blood runs in my own children. I am adept, after a decade and a half, at reading Carolyn's shorthand and brave enough to adapt each recipe to fit my own kitchen.

I no longer need to glance at my notes as I scald milk, add honey and salt, and pour it into the bowl to cool. I add oil, eggs, and wheat germ along with the frothing yeast that has already grown fat on more honey. Rye, whole wheat, and white flours bind the dough. I roll up my sleeves to wrestle and pound and find a rhythm while the sticking dough pulls away from the sides and becomes an elastic mass. When the kneading is done, I cover the bowl with a clean cup towel and step back.

———+—•—+———

My grandmother kept her bowls and her cooking tools hidden behind white cabinet doors. She had a ceramic cookie jar shaped like a monk with "Thou

Shalt Not Steal" written in white script across his fat belly. When I stuck my hand down into its depths, black crumbs of long-gone Oreos clung to my fingers, but I never found any cookies in the jar.

My grandmother's culinary specialty was a recipe that involved dipping raw chicken pieces in Hidden Valley Ranch dressing and then rolling them in crushed corn flakes that came in a box with a rooster on the front. During the week, tired from working all day at the bank in town, she made simple evening meals. She changed out of her suit and heels into sandals, shorts, and one of my grandfather's old white work shirts and sat on the porch swing with her drink in a plastic cup with a straw. On Sunday mornings, in her flowing housecoat with her hair still up in bobby pins, she made the chicken recipe. Later she clicked back through the kitchen in a straight skirt and high heels to turn the knobs on the oven to bake. She always wore a hat to church.

Thanksgiving at her house tasted like dip made from sour cream and Lipton's French Onion Soup mix. We ate on linen-covered card tables set with china, silver, and crystal, a confusing number of glasses and forks, and cloth napkins. Candles flickered in beaded-glass votives until, in midafternoon, we cleared the tables of their cloths to play forty-two or gin rummy to the tune of the football game on the television.

My grandmother cooked the turkey and provided the brown-and-serve rolls and the canned cranberry sauce. My aunt brought the sweet potatoes and the green bean casserole made with cream of mushroom soup and topped with french-fried onions. My mother made the cornbread dressing and giblet gravy, whisking briskly to keep lumps from forming while she thickened it with flour and scolded us to get out from under her feet. We waited anxiously for my mother's Aunt Patsy to arrive bearing the wonderful lead-up to the meal, the grazing tray, a work of art that she carried ceremoniously into the house and placed in the center of the red and white tablecloth. In the middle of that enormous lazy Susan would be a vat of french onion dip.

———•—•———

Bread Bowl

The heaviness of the dough contains the root of lightness. All the messiness, held in the smooth sloping walls of the pottery, gives way to uniformity—a whole new thing—this rising mound that lifts the cup towel into a dome. My fist sinks firmly into the center and the dough yields its empty spaces. In the deflation, there is the triumph of rising back up.

————•—•—————

My mother learned to make homemade flour tortillas from a bilingual maid named Josie who came to our house for one week the year I was ten. Her paycheck was signed by my grandfather. My youngest brother was born on a Sunday morning the weekend before the county stock show. During her fourth pregnancy, my mother had decided that she was not going to endure another hospital stay for a process as natural as childbirth. Any problems she had with the previous three births were either brought on or aggravated by hospital policies.

Her friend Corinne was a midwife who delivered many of the Hispanic babies in our town. She also delivered milk, eggs, and garden produce as well as making the best fruit leather I have ever eaten. She brought milk to our house in huge glass jars, yellow cream riding thick on the top. On the cold February morning that my mother went into labor, the neighbors took my brother and sister to the show barns to help wash hogs while I sat in the living room with my dad and a friend of my mom's and waited for news from the bedroom. Aunt Corinne was a huge woman. She held my mother's hands and stood with my mother's feet braced firmly on her thick thighs; together they pushed my new brother out onto the king-sized bed.

My grandparents were horrified. Childbirth belonged in the sterility of the hospital. New mothers should be treated as invalids. They didn't say a word about the natural-ness of it all, just pursed their lips and hired a maid to do housework for my mother for a week.

I went to school on Monday morning, though I would have preferred to sit cross-legged on the bed and watch the sweat bead up on the baby's bald head as he nursed. When I got home, the house was warm and smelled of baking powder. Josie was standing at the stove flipping perfectly round tortillas, and my mother was standing at the kitchen sink washing dishes.

My mother has always said that her skin isn't dark enough for her tortillas to turn out round like Josie's. She and I both make tortillas shaped like lily pads. My daughter carries on the tradition, wrestling with the heavy rolling pin, making the kitchen smell of baking powder, and flipping lily-pad-shaped tortillas on hot cast iron.

———•——•——

When the dough mounds again, I lift it in my hands and form loaves and rolls. The heat of the oven takes over the process, baking and browning the smooth tops. During the afterglow, and as the heavy, familiar smell fills the kitchen, I lift the bowl into the sink and fill it with hot soapy water to soak away the crusting remains of the dough so that it might be empty again, and waiting. Carefully, I wash it clean, rinse it, dry it, and return it to its place beside the flour canister. I take my time. One wrong bump, one careless slip, and the pottery form will be broken, its hollows never to be filled again.

Wounds

Back hooves and hocks are liberally coated with blood, bright red even though it has dried. The left front hoof and hock are in the same condition, suggesting an arterial spray. The right front leg hangs trembling, the toe gingerly brushing the ground. The cut, deep and slanting down into the hoof bed, is crusted over with dried blood mixed with horse pen dirt. The dun horse hangs his head while the boy halters him, and I open the gate to turn the other horses out of the corral, out of our way.

Oscar knows it is bad. But he keeps reassuring me in a voice that is high-pitched, strained, constant. Hunk, named after Sitting Bull's tribe, the Hunkpapa, pulls back on the halter rope, hesitating before each painful step, as we slowly lead him over to the water faucet. The boy fusses and scolds until the icy water begins running from the end of the green hose and over the wound. The ground around us turns to mud. Oscar hides his face against Hunk's neck, and we are silent.

Nick is on his way home, bringing vet wrap and wound salve and a promise that they will go straight to the vet, though he has already congratulated us, in a static-filled cell phone conversation. We did the right thing. Cold water is the best cure for a cut on a horse.

Still, this is not a company horse. This is Oscar's horse. They grew up together, this boy who wants to be mad at someone and this little horse with an attitude. The boy sits on the barn steps, holding the muddy lead rope between his knees while he eats meat and cheese wrapped in a homemade tortilla, carried out to him by Lily who tries to make him laugh. And they wait. They wait for the man who will make it all better, who will say, "Oh, it's not so bad! I've had worse than that on my eyeball!" For the man who will take charge of the wound.

———•—•———

"You never . . ."

"I always . . ."

"I knew it was going to turn out to be all my fault again."

The darkness does not hold any common ground. It is too full of words that flew from their mouths leaving disproportionate hollows behind. The bed is suddenly both too big and too small. She listens to his breathing and wonders if he is asleep. His hand lies heavy on his chest, impossible to lift and reach over to her hip where she lies curled away from him. Neither one of them moves during the night.

The smells of coffee and bacon, the unspectacular lightening in the east, the routine of letting the dog out and the cat in, the fact that one kid has an eye appointment and the other one has a birthday tomorrow, and she'll put her hand on his arm and he'll cover it with his own.

But later, as he pours out grain for the horses or takes a flat to town to be fixed, the words that hung in the darkness will echo back to him. As she makes the bed and carries their water glasses to the sink, she'll hear them, too, and her kids will wonder why she cries.

———•—•———

The mares in the small band no longer lift their heads from grazing when a dump truck rumbles across the cattle guard and down the pasture road. The stud, from his sentry post, looks up momentarily as it passes. In the center of the pasture, just where the land breaks from table-flat to rolling, a gaping hole in the ground breathes white dust out into the sky until a dew or a rain settles it all back into a crust. The yellow machine that dwells in the bottom of the pit breaks through the crust with its scoop-shovel jaw to take another bite and disgorge its load into the hungry trucks. Puffs of white dirt spiral up into the sky or skim across the grass or drift upwards into the almost still air. Each bite taken from the pit dislodges more grass root anchors, exposing the rocks and the white dirt below the surface, the caliche, the mineable hardpan.

Because of the wound, the land blows away or washes down the draw. The buffalo grass and broom weed and grama and bear grass inch slowly away from the crumbling cliff at the edge of the pit, their tenacity no match for the grazing machines, the construction project contracts, or the magic-wand dollars that opened the gates.

Someday, the trucks will stop coming. The cattle guard will itself be guarded by a gate with a padlock. The contract for mining the caliche in this pit will expire. Storm clouds will gather in the southeast to send out thunder and promise over the land.

Pause

He offered me a chance to stop. I almost missed it in my hurry, anxious to get my evening walk out of the way so I could bathe the day's sweat and garden mud off my body, eat some supper, and have time for a glass of wine on the porch before bed.

As I began my trek down the driveway, I saw him, standing still, silent, and regal in the shallow water in the dam below the house. Thinking the white egret would lift off and flap away out of sight at any moment, I stood and watched him. The sun still shone hot and bright enough that I had to squint as I looked down the road along the first stretch of my evening exercise, making my choice. He took one step and stayed, gazing down into the water. Turning away from the road, I stepped just as carefully through the weeds until I reached the shade of a mesquite tree on the opposite bank from him.

Pairs of hitched dragonflies performed the antithesis to ballet, dancing in the air and dipping down to touch the watery stage. In the shade, unpaired dragonflies flew up around me in a blue cloud before settling back to their grass-stem and mesquite-leaf barstools. In turn, they each made a choice of mate and joined the dancers over the water.

The egret, much larger than his cattle egret cousins, stood in the shallow water while the ducks sent out a welcoming committee, a little group of gossips headed his way. He said hello by standing on one leg, seeming to be motionless even when he moved, each step contemplated and each turn of his head graceful and smooth. Like a student at the feet of a wise schoolmaster, I ceased worrying about the time, the tasks, the trail. I paused.

A swallow took one last dip into the water for the night. Perhaps she was grabbing a wiggling insect to give her wide-mouthed children for a bedtime snack. Perhaps she needed one last daub of mud for her sculpture of the day to be complete. Perhaps she was thirsty after telling the sun good night. A bullbat made his first growling song into the evening air. The egret dipped his head quickly into the water, stretching his neck out to swallow before standing still once more. I rose from my seat to discover that the world had turned to shadow.

Ground Beef

Burlap sacks full of feed land whump, whump, whump on the flatbed of the pickup. One by one, Nick throws them from the door of the boxcar and then jumps in after them. He leans them up on their ends and rips back the strings along their tops. He lifts each hundred-pound weight, and the pelleted cake rattles into the top of the feeder. He folds each sack, gathers up the strings, and stows them in the boxcar. His black wool vest is covered with cake dust when he comes in the house for one more cup of coffee before heading out on his feed rounds.

The only green on the January prairie is in the bear grass. We need a heavy wet snow to knock down the broom weed that makes the steers' eyes water. As we sit on a rocky ridge overlooking a windmill down in the river bottoms, Nick counts silently, using his index and middle fingers to point at the steers drifting toward the sound of the horn. A trio of antelope stand to the west of the windmill below, watching with heads high. The steers begin to trot uphill as they catch the smell of the feed on the wind. They line out in a long string, the first ones cresting up over the rocks to stand, bawling, around the feed wagon.

"They look good, don't they?" I agree. They do look good for Mexican steers in midwinter. On a cow/calf outfit, camp men become familiar with the cows they feed year in and year out. They gather them spring and fall, wean their calves, and come to know them as personalities and characters. But the steer is itinerant, stepping off the truck in November or December, gone in October to feedlot, to rail, to box, or to burger. Still, every year a few steers make names for themselves.

Last year we had Duck, a steer with long black shaggy hair that hung down under his belly as if he had come straight from an English farmyard. It rained several inches in June, filling up the tank dam below the house. Duck stood in the water from June to mid-September, the only place where he could stay cool getting smaller and smaller around him. In the weeks before the trucks came, he stood on dry cracked mud, looking sad and over-heated.

The year before, we had a steer who looked like a bulldog with an under-slung jaw and beady little eyes. We talked of him with affection, not real-izing that he also must have had some sort of heart or respiratory deformity. He wasn't strong enough to make the gather during shipping and died when the cowboys roped him to pull him in the trailer.

Every year it seems that we end up with at least one steer raised as a pet down in Mexico. He sticks his head down in the feed sack while Nick is try-ing to open it and rubs up against the pickup expecting some attention.

This is my first time to go feeding with Nick this winter, and my first time to meet Wobbles in the McMurtry Pasture. As the cattle trot toward the feed truck in lines, in bunches, one by one, over the horizon and around the tank dam, I catch sight of a yellow steer making his way in a comical zigzag, carefully picking his way over rough ground, following the smell of his companions and the sound of the horn. He is blind. I also notice a steer who looks like he needs to be in a rehab unit. "Oh, that's the one I brought back from the dead," Nick says proudly.

———

Six weeks ago, as the sun shone hot into the cab of the feed pickup, I read my book in the magnified warmth while the cold wind carried the sound of the horn over the pasture. The heel of my hand pressed again and again into the middle of the steering wheel with no particular rhythm. From time to time I laid down my book, rolled down the window, and sat on the door to peer to the east at the cattle wandering ever closer to the promise of food. My son, on Hunk, circled to the north. My husband, on Skip-a-rope, circled to the south. They appeared and disappeared on the horizon, pushing, pushing, always pushing the cattle toward me. The steers already gathered around the suke wagon bawled in dismay at the lack of food forthcoming.

The cab of the pickup is dusty. A crusty spit cup rides in one of the cup holders, and an old Gatorade bottle full of water is in the seat along with extra coats and gloves and wild rags. Tally books are Velcro-ed to the sun visor: pasture counts, documented windmill repairs, and a list of mares ready to foal. A plastic buzzard, a Disney toy that Kipling wouldn't recognize, rides on the dashboard, perpetually cheerful. The backseat is full of hot shots, buggy whips, toolboxes, and a cardboard box of expensive medicine, syringes, and needles. A thick piece of pink chalk rolls around on the floor at my feet.

When the herd seemed to be gathered up closely enough, I closed my book, put the pickup in drive, and began to roll very slowly across the neighbor's pasture, green horse trailer bouncing along behind, followed by trotting steers (don't drive too fast), the men on horseback bringing up the rear. Across this pasture and through the wire gate and onto the farm-to-market road. In a long, messy line, we are headed to another part of the ranch. I pick up my pace, hurrying to get the animals off the pavement.

They trot behind, the clatter of cloven hooves a more even rhythm than my honking has been for the last half hour. A long honk with three short ones following. Quarter notes for several bars until a coda breaks the monotony, switching to eighth notes or even sixteenths until a whole note is merited, for we have reached the gate opened wide into the small trap south of the house. I pull through and onto the rough ground, bouncing a few yards to leave the gate free. And the lead steers stop—refusing to follow me through.

Slowly the men on horseback bring the whole herd into a bunch and begin pushing harder to get the leaders to spill through, off the highway. But the steers, discouraged by the lack of cake falling from the pickup, turn down the bar ditch. Nick lopes down the fence line. Skip-a-rope minces across the pavement, and they turn the leaders back. The whole herd balls up in front of the gate, and the morning comes to a halt.

I keep up the honking, though it doesn't seem to be doing any good. The cattle mill and slip on the back asphalt. The men raise their arms and bring them down hard on their leggings, slap, slap, slap. "Come on! Take the gate! Take the gate! Take the gate!" Oscar's horse slips on the pavement as he turns a steer back into the wad, fighting to keep his footing. The horn's rhythm takes on a frantic note as I struggle to breathe normally again. But something has to give, and soon a steer jumps over the imaginary barrier between the bar ditch and the pasture, and they begin to spill through.

I can cease honking as Nick waves me out of the gate and closes it behind me. My job is done. Oscar trots to the north corner of the trap to open that gate, and they will continue their back and forth pushing, taking the steers to the Big Pasture to spend the rest of the winter, all of the spring and the summer, until October when the trucks come to haul them away.

I head toward home to teach Lily's math lesson and brown the ground beef for the tacos we will eat for lunch.

———•—•———

"Move out of the way, Tiny," Nick growls as we circle another feed ground, this time in the Bull Pasture. A steer with very short legs scoots out of the way of the pickup wheels as the automatic feeder clangs open and shut, open and shut, and the counter mounted on the dashboard clicks. "That guy's parents may have been a bit too closely related," Nick comments as we pass a huge yellow animal with an enormous head and an overly docile look in his eyes.

At the last feed ground I meet Ralph. I have already heard tales of Ralph around the kitchen table. Ralph of the too-loose gray hide. Ralph, the bovine shar-pei. Ralph who walks to the feed ground like a fat old lady with a purse over her arm. He looks up at Nick's insistent honking as if to say, "But I *am* hurrying!" Nick speaks Ralph's name affectionately and cusses the other steers when they crowd him away from the line of cake on the ground. Ralph gets his own pile.

"Why isn't that one coming to feed?" I point to a black steer over by a windmill.

"Because he's stupid." We bounce across the pasture, his personal Meals on Wheels.

Up until a few weeks ago, not only did Nick load each 100-pound burlap sack onto the pickup bed, but he also walked each sack out, pouring long lines, like pinwheel spokes, away from the pickup with the cattle scattering around him. His knees ached at night. But now he has an automatic feeder mounted on this old truck. He can flip a switch and dump it out by the pound, driving big circles, while the steers line up in a spiral.

We drive over a ridge, and Nick lifts his left hand to begin counting the scattered steers down below. They lift their heads and trot or amble our way when they hear the horn. Nick reaches the end of his count and does some math in his head. "Hmph. Well, I overfed the last bunch then." He watches a lone steer up on the side of a hill who doesn't seem in a hurry to come eat. "Come on you stupid sonofabuck." He gives the horn an extra hard bump. "Big dummy." I wonder if he talks to himself when I am not along.

The sun is high overhead when we drive through the wire gate onto the highway and turn toward home. I hope the kids got their schoolwork done in my absence. A package of ground beef is thawing in the kitchen sink.

Every Horseman

Bleached cow skulls hang on the fences around the camp. Nick collects them while prowling multiple-section pastures where cows, bulls, and maverick steers evade men on horseback season after season, hiding in the brush until they die of old age. His booted foot scatters a mouse skeleton that lies on the feed room floor, each miniscule bone resting where gravity settled it as bacteria and time dissolved the fur and tissue. One week after we got married, he carried the coffin of Tee Richburg, a cowboy who rolled his pickup in the bar ditch between Roby and Rotan late one night. Yesterday, he fished a drowned hawk out of the reservoir.

Before Jack Frost was weaned away from the Pitchfork mare that bore him, the tips of his ears froze off in a blizzard, giving him the look of a comical teddy bear. All through the summer Nick rode the three-year-old colt, getting him ready to make fall works and bragging about him over supper. On a blistering Sunday in August we drove down the steep hillside to Croton Camp, glad, at first, to be home from the ranch rodeo in Wichita Falls. In front of the house, in a macabre still life, lay Jack Frost. His front hoof was caught between the bumper and the body of Nick's ranch pickup. He had kicked the whole passenger-side panel in, flattened the tire, and wallowed a big half-circle in the red dirt as he died. Flies buzzed over the loose manure behind Jack's tail and circled the deep indention where he had pounded his head in agony and bondage. Nick's shoulders heaved as he sat on the front stoop and read the story of Jack's last hours. It was the first time I ever saw my husband cry.

———•—•———

White and gray puffs of fur litter the front yard where the cats ate a cottontail rabbit in the night. The stench in the toy box turns out to be a horned toad that some kid stowed in a blue pencil box and then forgot about. Lily won't go with her dad to get oats anymore because he stomps the baby mice nested in the loose grain. Her favorite cat ate a nest of baby pigeons in the rafters of the hay barn yesterday.

———•—•———

Lily Rose was born while we were living in the east end of the Palo Duro Canyon on a JA lease along Mulberry Creek. Every year we calved out heifers from late December often until mid-June. By the time she was three, she had seen Nick assist in many births. She wasn't alarmed when a heifer banged around in the calving stall or squeezed his arm with her powerful pelvic contractions or bellowed in pain. She had seen the resulting shining wet calf that usually came in a rush after a certain point in the struggle, sliding out in a gush on the ground. She understood that sometimes it was necessary for Nick to push hard on a newborn calf's chest to get him to take his first breath or swing him by his back legs to drain the fluid from his lungs after a difficult birth. So how did she know that this calf was stillborn? Her screams and cries echoed off of the tin barn, and I had to carry her, sobbing, to the house. Three days later, the dogs found the carcass and dragged the hind legs up in the yard to gnaw on.

———•—•———

Every Horseman

The image on the ultrasound screen looked like a gummy bear, but it didn't pulse with a heartbeat and it rested too low in my uterus. A few hours later, it was gone, a lump of tissue discarded in the operating room. He fumbles for words, does chores that don't need doing, and can't understand why I am still crying. He died a small death himself when we left that Mulberry Creek country and moved up here onto the prairie above the caprock. He wished for a friend's death after a bad horse wreck, and cursed its absence as he helped that same friend's oxygen-starved, severely brain-damaged body with basic functions months later. He curses the meadowlarks that seem to have a death wish, flying up from the lush bar ditches to die on the grill guard of his pickup.

———•—•———

The rising sun glints off a million drops of melted ice on an intensely green wheat field. In the dark hours of morning, while Nick paced the kitchen and drank a whole pot of coffee, those drops of water were frost on the winter wheat. Now, he sits with the pickup windows rolled down and gazes at the pairs of legs sticking up all over the field. Six dead steers, bloated on the wheat that turned to poison with the heavy frost. He'll hook on to each carcass, drag it to the ditch, and call the rendering plant to haul them off. Then, he'll call the boss with a modified head count.

———•—•———

Last summer he disentangled the calico cat after it got hung up in the chain-link fence and died. He hangs coyote carcasses on the fence posts, but hates to see a doe that miscalculated her leap and died with her back legs tangled in the barbed wire. He fished a drowned baby chick from the water trough at the barn this morning. Somewhere, in the River Pasture, resting in the shade of a big mesquite tree, are the bones of a colt named Sugar Ray, stomped by rogue mares soon after his birth. Nick picked the colt's resting place after the vet put him down.

———•—•———

I am walking fast, my head bent, my arms swinging, ignoring the dogs running up ahead. Rather than enjoying the prairie or the exercise or the smells of a thousand damp plants, I am making a grocery list in my mind or planning a meal or finding just the right word for a sentence on my laptop. Those thoughts are gone as soon as I plant my foot firmly within three inches of a diamondback rattlesnake lying so flat on the ground that he looks as if he has already been skinned by a long knife and stretched on the barn wall to cure. I leap off of my planted foot, landing several feet on the other side. In midair I hear his brief warning buzz and know that I will dream of jumping over rattlesnakes for several nights to come.

———•———

Cradled in my palm, Nick's hand is solid and rough. I squint, trying to see the smallest cactus spines, picking them out with tweezers, one by one. Tomorrow a livid bruise will paint the inside of his knee where it hit the swells of his saddle as he was slingshotted out, away from the falling horse. He was riding the big tall sorrel he likes so much, checking waters in the Jog and the Bull Pastures. He had leaned over to come home when the horse stepped in a badger hole.

———•———

At the Gaslight Restaurant, we order sandwiches and salads, with bleu cheese dressing. A week ago, I hugged Nick and the kids good-bye and traveled up Highway 385 from Texas to South Dakota with my friend and mentor. In a few days, we'll retrace our steps. All week he's been the teacher, and I've been one of his students in a workshop on the creative process.

The silence is comfortable after the waitress leaves the table. She is tall, redheaded, intriguing. It is easy, after we begin our conversation, to talk of her rather than of the morning's assignment. He asked us to draw a line from who we are now to who we envision ourselves to be in the future.

Around the circle, the others in the workshop read of selling their art, signing contracts, of hot bright footlights. I chose instead a poetic description, and smugness.

The only time I get angry with him is when he tells me something I don't want to hear but know to be true.

He tells me that I need to see my art as a way to make a living. I turn my face away, my lips shut tight, when he mentions an old Spanish proverb:

Every horseman rides beside an open grave.

Family Tree

Tobacco juice ran down the creases beside his mouth. He sat on the edge of his rocking chair in the too-warm living room. I sipped Pepsi out of a jelly jar, my jaws stuck together with caramels from the glazed green candy bowl beside his chair. His voice was loud, and he put a hand up to adjust the volume on his hearing aids often. The words "San Simone Valley" took me beyond the room as he told about growing up in Arizona and selling horses to the U.S. Cavalry. He slapped his leg and sometimes hit the spittoon at the end of each story, his eyes not quite focused on the present. He told stories for hours on end when they were all he had left.

When no one was around to listen, he turned the baseball game up as loud as it would go, moving his chair closer and closer to the screen after he turned ninety.

When the names in his stories became slippery with years while the events remained clear and vivid, he turned to the rocking chair on his right. Through all of my childhood she sat crocheting and cross-stitching with crippled, bent hands, supplying the names in the breaks in his stories. In the end, he still turned his head to the right, and then looked back to his audience, bewildered. Her rocking chair was empty.

He owned a restaurant, a lumberyard, a reputation. He owned horses, every one of them a "cracker jack." He was a gambler who never rolled dice but wrote checks for truckloads of cattle, goats, or sheep, running them in the bar ditches until he sold them for a profit or found grass to lease. He always had a saddle for sale, or three. He bought and sold trailers, mules, horses, and opportunities. He drove a truck. He fathered five children. He wrote books.

At some point in my childhood I became aware of the black, long-bradded manuscript covers on the bottom shelf of the glass-fronted bookcase in our own living room. By the time I graduated from high school, I had read and reread the collection of short stories and both novels that my grandfather wrote. I knew his stories.

———·———

He spit Copenhagen juice into the dirt in the horse's shadow. I sat on the tailgate of an old brown pickup and watched him trim and rasp and shape and clinch. Sweat made a line that started between his shoulder blades and disappeared into the waistband of his Levi's. Sometimes I scraped manure and mud off of the old horseshoes and put them in the green five-gallon bucket in the bed of the truck, listening to the rhythm of his powerful arm, driving a nail into a hoof with two soft taps and four solid whacks, the tip coming out the wall of the hoof perfectly every time. He would twist off the sharp end, leaving a shining diamond of broken silver to be clinched on his next journey around the horse.

He threw out the television when I was in the fourth grade in an effort to promote reading and give us back the freedom of unstructured time. Now that he and my mother live alone, he owns a television so he can watch base-ball, muting the commercials and picking up the book at his elbow between innings.

My son follows him around and asks questions, listening to his Papa's stories and advice with careful attention. My daughter borrows from Papa's bookshelves, reading some volumes over and over. They are learning his stories.

He's been a rancher, a horseshoer, a student, a cowboy. In the 1980s, an oil company trained him to use sensitive instruments to test their wells. He was my senior English teacher and the first person I ever heard argue both sides of the abortion question equally well. He hunts arrowheads, studies ants, and views movies as art. He always has a saddle or trailer for sale, or three. He works at the sale barn on Mondays and Tuesdays. He fathered four children. He wrote a book.

I had been married for only a short time when he gave me the manuscript. Late that night I realized that my toes had been numb for two hours. Soft snores floated in from the bedroom where my new husband lay sleeping. The only light in the Croton River breaks of the Pitchfork Ranch was the one at my elbow, illuminating pages filled with my father's handwriting on the table in front of me. It was a new day before I turned the last page, tucked my cold feet up under me, and stacked the unbound sheets neatly, title page on top.

> *Blue Chambray*
> *by Tom Hale*

Last I heard, the manuscript was still in his handwriting.

———•———

The house at Davis Camp on the JA Ranch was drafty, with few windows to let in the light. It was twenty miles to town, twelve of them over red dirt roads that were rough when they were dry, slick and boggy when they were wet. Old phone lines snaked across the pastures, poles broken off, wires sprung loose into hoof-catching masses. Cell phone towers were still too sparse to do us much good.

And so, the kids and I moved to Egypt one fall. Curled up on the bed we read about pyramids, the Sphinx, a holy cat who lived in Bubastes, petroglyphs, pharaohs, and mysteries. In the spring, we dove under the ocean and tangled the bedroom in kelp and fishnet hung with dried, stiff starfish and sand dollars, doing math to the sounds of whales singing to one another on the CD player, while the wind blew the Panhandle dirt from county to county. We spent time in Mitford, in Redwall Abbey, at Hogwarts, learned character lessons with Little Britches, and camped on an island in the Lake District of England with the Swallows and Amazons. I read aloud from Alcott, from Frost, from piles of books hauled home from the library. We read aloud "The Ransom of Red Chief" and *Cheaper by the Dozen,* always warning each other to go to the bathroom first.

———————

It is nothing that a seven-dollar bucket of white paint won't remedy. Her walls are covered with scrolls and turquoise flowers, her name, geometric designs and graphic elements in primary colors. She cut up one of my good sheets to make a canopy over her bed. I find scraps of pink and red paper with loving messages written on them tucked under my pillow or in my book or taped where I will see them when I go into the kitchen. At age ten she is preparing to start her first cottage industry, Two Flowers Teas, a lily and a rose entwined on the logo. She stores her herbs in Ziploc bags, creating and testing each blend before spooning it into heat-sealable tea bags and ironing them shut. Her sewing basket is a jumble of fabric scraps and tangled embroidery yarn, but she's made a heating pad for everyone in the family. She fills them with popcorn kernels and mint leaves so that they come out of the microwave aromatic and warm. She plays the comic relief in the duet performances she and Oscar stage in the grass on summer evenings. She writes science reports about the field mice burrowed beneath the prairie, their hollows lined snug against the bitter cold. She writes poetry in her journal, and sometimes I get to read it.

———————

The books he leaves lying about have lurid covers, fanciful cities and dragons and sword-wielding women warriors in other-worldly armor. On the shelf beside his bed is every book that Will James wrote. His alarm rings early and he comes into the kitchen dressed in Wranglers and denim shirt and cow shoes, pours his coffee, says good morning, and spends an hour doing push-ups, working on his algebra, or learning to tie a new knot with rawhide, the heavy instruction book propped beside the chair in his room, his awl close at hand. A rope strung across his bedroom is threaded with fifteen halters, the product of his winter afternoons. He'll sell them or trade them off, sitting on the tailgate swapping bits and spurs and gear with men who used to go easy on him, teaching the button to trade. He skinned a dead steer last week and nailed the hide to the barn wall to cure. Yesterday I saw him, sitting astride the silver cylinder of the water trailer, the hide draped across its fat arc. Hair flew from beneath his knife as the poem he was reciting flew away in the wind. When it is his turn to choose the music that we clean house to, he has a hard time choosing between Ian Tyson and Led Zeppelin. Today, he recited "Where the Ponies Come to Drink" and "The Shallows of the Ford," poems by Henry Herbert Knibbs that slowed my morning down to a fine chill and a choked throat, an unexpected gift. He's preparing for the poetry gathering where he'll do the same for audiences who don't know him like I do. It's his turn at the computer right before lunch. He double-clicks on an icon labeled "Oscar's Book." He's working on the third chapter.

——•——

My father is prowling my living room, looking through the books on my shelves. I go to my antique desk where my laptop is glowing and gather up E. B. White, *The Rural Life, Magpie Rising*. I know he doesn't like female writers.

Back in the living room, I kneel beside him. He has chosen a Sam Brown novel. A red plastic cup with a paper towel stuffed inside rests on the arm of the chair. He spits in it before he looks up. Before I can get two sentences out, explaining that I have been reading a lot of essays lately, he cuts me off.

"Twinkie, I don't like to read essays. I didn't even enjoy teaching them to my students. I've got to have something with a story." He waves the western at me before resuming his page.

Handmade Life

He wears a sweat-stained silver-belly hat and six-year-old Tony Lama boots. His bowed legs are encased in faded Levi's riding low on his hips. A dented thermos rides beside him in the seat year 'round. His trailer rattles, and his pickup is held together with baling wire and cussedness.

He has ridden the same saddle for forty years. It was new when he left for the war. Still wearing his uniform, he pulled it from the rafters of his mama's garage three years later. It was no longer shining with newness but caked with dust and cobwebs. The leather was dry-rotted and mice-chewed. In those first silent days he oiled every inch and replaced the crumbling latigos and stirrup leathers. He took it to the saddle shop on the square to be relined. His next stop was the bank where the GI Bill got him a loan to buy what his kids call the "home place."

During the war, the cows in the sale rings were cheap with no young men left to work the big outfits. He remembers those first few weeks after he got out of the service as if he were standing on a ridge between heaven and hell. He surveyed his life and bid on the future. The first signs of hope for him were the saddle and the pretty girl he danced with in the Legion Hall. She makes good coffee.

He's made their living tied to banknotes and weather and markets. In the good years he pastures cattle for other people along with his own cows. In the dry years he shuts the gates and watches the sky. He expanded the borders of the home place, and for the past several years he has leased the three sections across the highway. He's ridden every inch of fence line more than once. He knows the inner workings of each windmill as intimately as he knows his wife's body. Last year he shipped a broad-muzzled old tiger-striped cow. Old hussy had no business having a calf at her age. He sold the best horse he ever owned when the cow market was bad.

The only time his eyes fill with tears is when one of his children walks across the stage to receive a college degree. None of them will come back here to live and work. They'll make their own way. This is his life, built with his hands, to his specifications. He stoops to unbuckle the worn Oscar Crockett spurs he bought off of the feed store wall forty years ago. When he isn't horseback, they hang by their leathers from his saddle horn. His wife and children gave him a new pair of silver-mounted spurs for Christmas last year. They hang on the wall, the silver shiny under a thin layer of dust.

———•—•———

The smell of Cut-Heal mingles with the smell of dirt stirred up by the horses chewing grain as the horizon begins to show pink. A commotion at the far end of the bunk stirs up more dust. Even in the dark he knows that Keystone is the one causing the ruckus. The cowboy, leaning in the open door of the saddle house, wears a black felt hat with a taco crease. His Levi's are tucked into tall boots with stovepipe tops and big-rowled gal-legs on the heels. When the horses finish eating, he catches the one named Booger Red.

The sky is a washed-out blue as he tosses his handmade saddle on the horse's back. It is completely rigged out with Pointer hardware, right down to the oxbows adorned with silver poinsettias and copper leaves. He chooses the Sprayberry bit, one of several bridles hanging on the wall. Booger Red, hard-mouthed and aggravating as hell, wears a company brand on his shoulder that matches the one painted on both the red trailer and the automatic feeder mounted on the flatbed of the pickup. It is echoed on the entrance to this camp and on the left hips of the cows he will prowl this morning. His paycheck bears the same brand.

He unrolled his bed at the Pitchfork wagon the day after he graduated from high school, and he's been working for big outfits ever since. As a boy, he listened to the old men tell stories of the days when their only possessions were a change of clothes, a bedroll, and their kack, when they moved from bunkhouse to bunkhouse, lived from payday to payday, roped wild cattle out of the river breaks, and never checked up. He got a small taste of that life in the beginning, though he owned a pickup and had to make a bigger circle. Still, he has some stories of his own now and has lived on some great camps.

The country he looks after isn't his. He doesn't choose the breed of cows that graze the pastures or the lineage of the horses he rides. He doesn't choose when to pick up bulls or how many heifers to keep. He doesn't choose the pickups he drives or the type of hay he feeds his horses. He doesn't choose how much day help to hire or the shipping dates in the fall. He doesn't fret about weights or numbers or the scheduling of trucks and vets.

He does choose who makes his boots, spending long Saturday afternoons in the boot shop, poring over leather catalogs, drawing underslung heels on brown paper, and making sure the boot maker knows exactly what he wants—French calf bottoms, colorful tall tops, tear-drop pull holes, stove-pipe or scalloped, row after row of stitching in fancy patterns. He chooses the silver on his bits and spurs—a card hand, a rattlesnake, a simple flower with leaves, a steer skull, a brand, a gal's leg with garter and high heels. He chooses the rowels, the shanks, the headstall buckles. He chooses the length of his chaps, the thickness of his saddle pad, the shape and color of his hat. He has a growing collection of bits made by a man named Klapper.

Last Sunday he sat and spit with a trading buddy over two piles of plunder, both piles growing and shrinking through the afternoon. His buddy's dreams of owning his own place and being his own boss reminded him of a time seven or eight years ago when he and his wife stood at a crossroads. They questioned whether or not to look for a new ranch job or rent a trailer house and five acres on the edge of town. The second option meant day working, shoeing horses, and riding two-year-olds for other people, thirty days at a time. Or, if that didn't bring in enough money, she mentioned that he could always go to work for the carbon black plant or train to be a guard at the prison. When this camp came open, he shook hands with the cow boss and made the deal. It took him two days to get this saddle house cleaned out and organized. It took him eight days to prowl every section of the country that goes with the camp. It took him thirty days to leg up his string of horses.

The sun is already hot, and the dew is beginning to dry on the grasses as he jumps his horse in the trailer and slams the gate shut.

———·•·———

Most people woke to the buzz of an alarm this morning. They put on suits and ties or heels and hose and drove through the rumble and exhaust of morning traffic to the tempo of stoplights and merging lanes. They punched a clock or said hello to receptionists in front of ringing phones. They shuffled papers, attended meetings, and composed e-mails about impending projects or seminars. They ate lunch at cluttered desks or worked out at the gym. They got their nails done or bought a new laptop. They closed deals and used public restrooms and drank coffee out of cardboard cups. They were happy or sad or busy or bored.

This morning I woke with my head facing east before the sun came over the horizon. I put my tin pot full of water over last night's coals and drank my coffee from an enamel mug. I started my day to the rhythm of the waking-up prairie while a few nosy clouds gave the sun's location away. Their bottoms caught fire, and they dissolved while the red sun banished the shadows.

Today I hiked through sage and thistle and bear grass. I gathered dry cow patties for my evening fire. I squatted to pee in the dirt and rocks. I ate lunch in the sliver of shade still left beside the range tipi and watched the ants tote off my crumbs. I read my book. I wrote things down. I stood for long moments and looked off over the land under a sky so big it made my heart hurt. I sat on an upturned bucket and did nothing, thought nothing, said nothing. I read aloud to no one. I stepped on a tortoise who made a sound like a wet bath toy. I cut open a prickly pear with my knife. I ate a melted Hershey bar and wiped my hands on my jeans. I watched the clouds make shadows on the land. I sweated. I drank tepid sun tea because I had no ice. I stepped in yesterday's footprints in the pasture road as I made my way to the windmill, noting that many of my old tracks were already overlaid with those of birds, rabbits, mice, coyotes, and insects. I splashed in the water and brushed my teeth in the narrow stream coming out of the lead pipe. I floated on my back and let my hair drift around me. I walked back to camp slowly to keep from sweating. I cooked bacon and summer squash over hard-won coals. I drank red wine and watched a full moon rise. I apologized profusely to the tortoise, but he didn't forgive me.

Tomorrow I return to alarm clocks, e-mail, telephones, and demands. Everything I do will be in light of this time alone on the prairie, stolen away from the daily life of meals, kids, and chores. Everything I do is so that I might return to this place. Everything I do must be toward a handmade life, custom-building my days out of the fabrics of my choice.

Fourth of July

All evening long, the rodeo arena was a glittering snow globe, the tall lights reflecting off of the dust stirred up by men, cattle, and horses. It is empty now except for three little boys popping firecrackers in the deep red dirt. The action has moved to the dance floor where the band is loud, and terrible, but the dancers don't care. In pairs, they shuffle around in a circle to the beat coming out of hulking black speakers. Off to one side, I spot my daughter's braid swinging from side to side, the braid I made quickly as we stood in front of the mirror in my bedroom. She is doing a jerky, mechanical two-step with a miniature cowboy. One, two, one. One, two, one.

The cinder-block restrooms are marked COWS and BULLS in faded black letters, and the Boy Scouts sell hamburgers, chili dogs, and cans of cold Dr. Pepper long into the night. The sheriff is parked under a street lamp, and three watchful men in uniform lean on the hood of his car. Groups of people drift toward the music and lights; pairs drift back out into the shadows. Mosquitoes swarm up out of the grass as the night cools. The smells of summer, hamburgers cooking over mesquite coals, ammonia mixed with arena dirt, and sulfur from the Black Cats fill the air.

Many of the married couples keep their five dollars in their pockets and stand outside the chain-link fence beneath the nonbearing mulberry trees.

They have wooed and won at previous dances. Now they visit with friends and watch new stories unfold. Young girls walk by in groups of two or three, neon cell phones in their hands. They don't wear Levi's or Wranglers anymore, preferring Cruel Girl or Petrol or Hollister. Groups of five or six young men move around with much less grace and much more noise, leaving a reeking wake of cologne. One young man whose cologne was long ago obliterated by horse sweat and arena dirt gathers the most girls around him. He made a good showing on his uncle's ranch rodeo team, milking the cow and running the longneck bottle to the judge standing in the white chalk circle to win the wild cow milking event. Now, he's standing tall, cloaked in the admiration of his buddies. Later, I see him walk off into the dark with a slim young woman beside him.

The band plays on, asking the crowd's forgiveness when it leaves country and western behind for a thumping version of AC/DC. My son, wearing a red shirt just like my husband, comes over to the chain-link fence to ask for a bottle of water. He points out the three girls he has been dancing with. He has known two of them since they were all three years old, playing in the wading pool in their underpants. One of them has braces on her teeth and the other has a pimple on her chin, but he doesn't seem to notice. The third girl is from out of town and she wears a T-shirt emblazoned with "Red, White, and Boys." A group of four or five ranch boys in hand-me-down boots are keeping the girls busy, shoving them around the dance floor awkwardly, all elbows and knees and hats.

The evening's entertainment was a ranch rodeo with teams of men from all over this end of Texas coming to compete. Faces from every era of my life appear out of the darkness to shake hands and say hello. It is standard in the cowboy world to ask a man if he still likes his job and how the outfit in general is doing. Over and over, we are asked about the man we work for. Many of the cowboys have worked for him at some point in their lives, usually when they were young enough and salty enough to ride the pitching horses he raises.

Two cowboys I've known for a decade rib each other for being quitters. One of them just moved onto a ranch camp south of here, and the other is renting a house in town and day working. The more talkative one fills us in on the new owner of the ranch they just left. He tells us about big money and big changes, the dispersal of a well-respected horse-breeding program, and the efforts of the foreman to make the transition as easy as possible for the cowboys, even though he himself chafed under the new policies. Mention of the foreman's name makes every man look up, and the volume coming from our group increases as each man agrees with the highest compliment a cowboy can offer: *He's a cowpuncher.* None of these men holds the new policies against the foreman, but when the storyteller mentions that the cowboys on the ranch are now limited to three head of horses, every man looks at the ground, spits, and utters an expletive. They mutter about idiots in offices who think that a man can make spring or fall works with only three horses under him.

"But that wasn't why I quit." The quiet man speaks. "For two years I have been meeting the school bus every afternoon to get my kid. My wife works in town. The foreman knows I do my job, and when we are working with the crew, I always come right back . . . just bring him with me." I've seen this homely, common, unremarkable man ride a bucking horse out of the chute. I've seen him a hundred times standing on the fringes of a noisy crowd, just listening. This is the most I have ever heard him speak. "I quit because they don't allow kids to help on the ranch anymore. I had to trot off and leave my boy behind, him just abawlin'. What's the point?"

A group of little boys runs past us, ropes in hand. One of them catches another around the ankles, and the whole group goes down in a big wad. What's the point?

"Cotton-Eyed Joe" filters through the darkness. It's after midnight, and I send my daughter to tell my son that as soon as the song is over, he is to get with us so we can head home. To the west, someone begins shooting off fireworks. A tired horse wakes from his nap beside a trailer and pulls back on the lead rope. A beer can crumples, and a cooler lid slams. A limp, wilted toddler in a formerly white eyelet shirt sleeps against her daddy's shoulder, pink boots dangling. The women standing around me are getting quieter, but the men just get louder and more prophetic, profane, and profound.

Our kids are asleep in the backseat before we leave the lights of town behind. My husband and I drive in silence through the dark. The old man sleeps hundreds of miles away to the north . . . the old man who owns the ranch where we live, the old man who cares about people more than policies, the old man who holds it all together, the old man who would never limit a man to three head of horses and who called our son last fall, inviting him to be one of the crew during shipping.

The old man is ill. Sky lightning ripples in the north.

Fourth of July

Out of the Blue

A battered blue trampoline, torn from its moorings, leans tiredly against the barn where the wind flung it two weeks ago. A broken glider swing rests on its nose amidst torn and water-damaged cardboard boxes. Flies hover and stick over a garbage can stuffed with the spoiled contents of the refrigerator and freezer that now hum in her new house. The stench of rot is strong.

The open nose of the horse trailer is almost full, stacked with leather, nylon, and silver. Two horses stand tied, stamping and sleeping, waiting to be loaded. A cowboy walks out of the saddle house where he is packing up his gear and drinking beer. He says hello with a big smile and a hearty wave, but there is a flavor of shame and despair in his conversation. The story reel that we have been listening to for over a month continues to unwind as we join him in the cool dimness of the barn, but now it is stuck on refrain.

She's tired of footing the bill. She wants the security of a retirement plan and regular vacations. She's tired of moving around, tired of him being gone, tired of beef. Their married years are a blur of horses, dogs, new saddles, thirty-day budgets, and grand plans. The day working makes her tired, but so did the steady ranch jobs. They were only good for about six months, before his bitching started. Her daughter has attended two different schools already, and she'll only be a second grader this fall. The daily danger, the rowdy friends, and the poor pay pale in comparison to the day-to-day mundane grind of her job in town and life with a man who is gone for days on end, day working for ranches within a five hundred mile radius. She's tired of holding it all together. Maybe she's tired of him.

He shakes his head and swipes his hand over his mustache. This whole thing hit him out of the blue. *Out of the blue.* He did all he could do. He tried his hardest, and can't imagine what more she wants from him. What about his little girl? He tips the silver can and turns his face away.

———•—•———

She's just a woman. Ranch-raised or a girl from town, educated or waiting tables at the café. She plants a garden and builds furniture out of barn wood, or she sits and watches soaps and is an eBay queen. She's sweet and soft or rough-talking and hard. Tall or short, she's simple and complicated. Blonde or redheaded, determined or confused, spoiled or content, scared that when she gives up on him, she gives up her whole circle of friends in the cowboy world.

He's just a cowboy. He wears a sweated-through straw hat, but it might as well be black or silver. He drinks Coors Light, but it might as well be Budweiser; he gets loud and red-faced when he drinks too much. He's a good hand with a horse, maybe too impatient and rough sometimes. He ties hard-and-fast outside, but dallies in the branding pen. Mustache or clean shaven, sinner or saint, cigarettes or snuff, soft spoken or blowhard, strong work ethic or drifter, married, single, or divorced.

———•—•———

It started out amicably with both parties mentioning Gracie, their little girl, repeatedly, speaking of how to make this easier for her. Now he talks about getting his own lawyer so he won't get screwed and selling a box of collectible bits and spurs to a friend for $100 so that *she* won't wind up with them. He's moving in with a buddy. She squirreled away enough money for first and last month's rent in a good school district close to her job. I don't mention the hours she sat at my kitchen table weighing her options, and no one mentions the evening a couple of weeks ago when he sat on our front porch, his tears flowing in the dark.

He wonders aloud if there is still hope—if she will take him back. The silence in the saddle house sits heavy while the breeze blows the stench off the garbage and into the open door.

———•—•———

The next day I drop the kids off at the swimming pool and take my pickup over to the service station. A taillight is out, so I sit in the shade amidst the din of the tire machine and men working while a local high school boy changes the bulb. I think about our friends and the fragmentation of their lives. A pickup pulling a horse trailer with the words "Cowboy Outreach Ministry" painted on the top goes by on Highway 287. I realize that in all of the talking I have heard over the past month, I have not heard the word love.

Rightful Place

64

Reserves

Cold tea sloshes in the mason jar, and the bottom of the glass numbs my thigh below the hem of my shorts. Sometimes a bump in the rough road splashes tea up over the rim, small paisley shocks. The heat rises up off the land in midday.

Nick stops at a wire-and-post gate in the east/west fence line, puts the pickup in park, and slams the door behind him. The tail of his dingy white shirt is uncharacteristically untucked. His strides are long, and he grips the posts firmly, one big shove loosening the wire enough to slip the gate free, but I can tell from the set of his shoulders that he is tired. There is stubble on his face and concrete dust on his black hat. For two weeks he has driven these two simple lines, snaking off to the northeast, over and over and over. We are headed to a windmill so that I can see what he has been doing.

When I was a little girl, I loved to leave town in my dad's ranch truck and head out along Highway 54 north of Van Horn, Texas, to spend the day with him on the ranch. I loved fencing or checking water, eating our lunch out of the black lunchbox and drinking soft drinks out of the cooler. Sometimes my dad taught me Spanish nouns as we drove along: *conejo, caballo, vaca, alambre, paisano.* My favorite word was *papalote.* He explained that *papalote* means both "kite" and "windmill." I don't think he knew that the first meaning is from the Karankawa Indian word rather than Spanish, but the imagery was still the same for me.

Up here on the prairie, the windmill, that holdover from the past that still blesses the land with each turn of its fan, is only as good as its storage. This close to the Salt Fork of the Red River, water pumped into dirt tanks or dams simply seeps back into the sand, returning to the bedrock to sit in sweet useless silence. The rancher must find a way to store the water that rides upward on the checks when the winds blow so that when they cease, the cattle can still drink. This pasture is in desperate need of more storage, so for two weeks my husband has been leveling the site, digging a heel-fly pond and welding the actual steel that will encase the water. Yesterday, concrete trucks bounded over the ranch road and a crew from another division came to help set the reservoir. All of the labor is well spent because last summer Nick hauled load after load of water to this location when the wind wasn't blowing and the steers stood bawling with thirst in the dust beneath the tower.

The landscape is altered here at the mill. Rather than two small rusted brown tubs with tall cattails growing in the centers, the windmill swings over a new obscenely silver cylinder. The windmill truck sits like a dead bug amidst the detritus of two weeks' labor. An empty paint can, testifying to the origins of the glaring silver, lies forgotten on its side in the dirt. A hot wire is strung around the site to keep the cattle from marring the fresh concrete and paint, and my husband warns me that it is indeed hot as I get ready to duck under it. A steady stream of water flows from the lead pipe into the slowly filling reservoir, but the cowboy shakes his head in dismay at how little the water has risen in its depths since he trotted up here on a bronc in the cool of the morning. The evaporation rate is high in this heat, and the windmill can only pump as many strokes as the wind will allow.

I stand on a ladder, looking over into five inches of water covering a circle twenty-three feet in diameter. Nick stands beside me, easily peering over the five-foot sides, and telling me about its construction with measurements and numbers that come easy to him. When he sees what might be a hole in the fresh concrete, I pull off my shoes and socks and get on his shoulders while he lifts the ladder over into the interior. It's a precarious climb. I wade across the newly stored commodity to check the rough floor for flaws.

Twenty miles south of here, water pumped up out of the ground contains gypsum, a mineral that eats steel and concrete and must be held in fiber-glass instead. The gyp will eat a person's insides as well, or make one wish it would do the job faster rather than by slow, dehydrating, gut-wrenching means. I am glad the water flowing out of this pipe is sweet. I put my tongue in the stream, but opt for commitment when I open my mouth for a good splashing gulp. My shirt dries quickly in the June heat, but the memory of that cold water causes me to look wistfully back at the meager depths as I climb out and onto his shoulders again. At some point I will come back to this clear reserve of water, when it has filled to the brim, truly kept for cattle, but secretly kept for my swim. Maybe in the moonlight.

On our roundabout return journey, we bounce across the pasture, lush after a wet spring, but showing signs of wear after these last few hot days. The steers, standing belly-deep and bored, are too lazy to move out of our path as they switch at flies and exchange pleasantries with the heifers across the barbed wire. The *M* branded on their right hip makes me wonder if they ever saw so much food in their previous lives, south of Juárez. That water I waded in is for them.

My tea is not as cold now. I sip it down to the bottom of the jar as the house comes in sight.

Harvest

A blue heron stands atop the light pole at the barn. He surveys the camp without turning his head. The shipping pens down below are an empty grid. The rank, dense weeds that filled them in summertime have been trampled and crushed by hundreds of hooves. Crusted-over piles of cow manure make hazardous islands in the deep dust along the alleys and up the ramp to the loading chute. The kicked-up powder that hung in the air a few days ago has settled back to earth. The barn lots and hay racks are empty, but a grey and a sorrel graze companionably on the back side of the horse trap, pieces of remuda left behind when the cowboys moved on to the next ranch. One red steer gazes mournfully into the water trough. He went visiting the neighbors and missed the last truck to the feedlot.

The land is tired. Its productivity has peaked and fallen. Cool, foggy mornings give way to long afternoons of hot winds that cure the grasses, turning them yellow and silver and ivory. Beneath the old heat is a hint of change, a precursor of the land's resting time. The garden smells of decaying leaves, dried cucumber vines, and too-ripe tomatoes. The trees in the creeks are giving up their green, gold rattling amidst the branches. The air is hazy, and the gayfeather is blooming, purple and dusty. Most of the dirt tanks are dry, and the coyotes' chatter gets louder each night as they come closer to the house for water.

Wasps swarm around the windowsills in the warm afternoons. The wind chimes never stop moving. The morning glory leaves are macabre valentines with black lace edges, while the mums glow orange and yellow from the first touch of frost. The ranch dog sleeps in a patch of sun, the ruff of his neck stained green where he rolled in cattle truck sludge. The barn door is closed, and the saddle racks are empty, though the smells of gall salve and peanut oil linger.

———·•·———

Two weeks ago Nick frowned in concentration, studied his tallies, made phone calls, and moved cattle, horses, and loading chutes around the ranch. I washed bedroll blankets and pulled musty brush jackets, wild rags and wool vests from the hall closet, just in case. The freezers and refrigerators were full of groceries and ice, and I carried the five-gallon tea jug and forty-cup coffeepot up from the cellar. The calendar was free of superfluous marks, no doctor's appointments, play dates, camping trips, or ranch rodeos to mar the white squares reserved for the culmination of the year's work. The fat steers in the pastures were the only ones not looking down the road, listening for the rigs bringing cowboys and bosses.

A week ago the camp rang with unfamiliar spurs and the racket of horses being unloaded out of trailers with wooden floors. The saddle house was crowded with too many saddles, feed buckets overturned for chairs, and men telling stories with ropes in their hands. The house smelled of beef roasting slowly in the oven, beans bubbling in the slow cooker, and bread dough rising or baking. The barn lot echoed with squeals and thumps as horses established rank in the temporary pecking order. The men drank beer out of silver cans at the barn and iced tea out of red plastic cups at the house.

The mornings smelled of coffee, frying bacon, and fog. Before the sun came up, the men sat quiet and straight in their chairs waiting for the biscuits to brown in the oven. I walked out into the first filtered light of day to scatter scraps for the chickens as the cowboys mounted up and trotted out, damp air magnifying the sounds of creaking leather, ringing rowels, and fresh horses firmly in hand. The truckers who slept in the lane all night, motors idling and heaters running, came in for coffee. They ate leftover scrambled eggs and cream gravy while I peeled green apples and fluted the edges of the pie crusts.

The days were full of the hiss of air brakes, the slam of trailer gates, and the rattle and rush of cattle as they moved beyond the cowboys' shouts and onto the decks. Once loaded, the trucks groaned away from the chute while the steers shuffled and shifted, finding their footing for the long ride. Dust fogged up from the road as the trucks moved down the lane and onto the highway. The door to the house opened and shut as cowboys came and went, conferring with the boss, removing their hats respectfully, but leaving footprints of dirt and manure on the linoleum and carpet. The boss spoke quietly into the phone to men in feedlot offices, banks, and Mexico, arranging for fresh cattle to arrive this winter while the steers left in the pens outside bawled and milled, waiting for the trucks to double back. I did the same math that so many women before me have done—women cooking for harvesting crews, threshing crews, railroad crews, shearing crews, and cowboy crews—but like them, I still added a couple more potatoes to the pot, just to be sure.

In the evenings, the men rocked back in their chairs, lingering at the supper table over one more slice of pie and a rehash of the day. Someone joshed the kid as he put more beans and bread on his plate. They all wish they could eat as much as he does and still get on their horses.

———————

Oscar tightens the leather straps around his bedroll and stuffs one last jacket in his duffel bag. He stomps, heavy-laden, through the kitchen, stopping to grab a leftover biscuit out of the bowl. His spurs sound like his dad's.

With the dishwasher humming and the leftovers stored in the refrigerator, I lift the brown paper sack of perishable groceries that I didn't use up this week. I'd rather the cook at the next ranch use them than let them spoil in the silent days to come. I carry the sack out to Nick's pickup and stay to watch the loading up. Oscar's three-year-old bronc, Cody Blue, shakes his head vigorously and sets back when the cowboys try to coax him into the close confines of the crowded gooseneck. The air fills with dust and impatient curses, until someone puts the loop of a lariat rope around Cody Blue's rear, and he jumps nimbly in to stand beside a sorrel who hasn't even looked 'round at the commotion. The trailer gate clangs shut, and my husband ties it firmly with a piggin' string.

The boss's Cadillac pulls onto the dirt road, and every rig, loaded with bedrolls, saddles, and men, inches slowly in the same direction. Two years ago Oscar stood beside me, fighting to keep from crying, every ounce of him aching to join the cowboys as they headed to the next division. Today he waves at me from the passenger seat before turning his eyes forward to the road. I wave back, and the cowdog leans against my legs. I can see Lily up on the haystack, watching from the shadows. As Nick's pickup and trailer pull into the line of moving vehicles, she jumps down and comes running to stand at my side, her arm around my waist. When the last rig turns right onto the pavement, we turn together to go into the house to face the dirty floors and the quiet. Above me, up in the blue, I hear the calls of the geese for the first time. They are moving south, high and fast.

———•—•———

The house smells like the harvest spice candle burning on the kitchen table. There are no boots or spurs on the floor under the coat hooks in the mudroom and no manure-smeared Levi's in the laundry basket. I spent the afternoon scrubbing the hummingbird feeders and moving the geraniums and bougainvilleas into the house for the winter. The only light shining in the dusk is the one beside Lily's bed where she is sprawled, reading a book with a dragon on the cover. For three days we have eaten leftovers out of the refrigerator, slept until we woke after dawn, and made cups of hot tea for each other.

Tonight the moon is fat on the horizon. Coyote pups wrestle and nip at each other at the bottom of a maroon cut bank. Their mother lopes up out of the draw and points her nose in a song that sails out over the prairie. Later she'll bring fat quail and drop them at the half-grown pups' feet. After their supper she'll teach them a rapid staccato yip while the feathers drift away on the breeze. But her mind is on her burrow, for the wind has a bite right before dawn, and she knows how deep a Llano Estacado winter can be. Along the highways, deer lift their heads from grazing in the too-tall grass to gaze into the headlights of each passing car. A buck gathers his legs beneath his belly and sails against the moon, barbed wire an incidental annoyance in this month when he is king. At a lonely windmill, water spills over into the heel-fly pond for the first time all year. A pair of antelope wait to drink until after dark, the smell of cattle still strong around the tubs.

I sit in my chair on the front porch, wrapped in a sweater, my knees drawn up. The red steer bawls for his long-gone companions, a coyote sends up yips to the south, and a heron's form floats down to the creek while my Walmart wine glass turns to crystal.

Bling

My arms are full of folded white cotton T-shirts and my mother's satiny nightgown, sweet smelling from the dryer. I rest my chin on the pile and turn the knob of my parents' bedroom door. The room is dim and quiet, the bed neatly made. The sewing machine in the corner of the room is piled with a garment under construction, crinkly tan pattern pieces pinned to the wrong side of the fabric. I lay the clean laundry on the dresser.

My mother's jewelry chest is covered in muted-gold fabric. I lift the lid and run my fingers over her treasures. My favorites are the lapel pins stuck in the satin lining, a faded green beetle with minute rhinestones marching up the crease of his shell, a gold fox with an emerald eye, a mass of silver filigree framing a stone-white cameo with a red rose in the center.

I lift her charm bracelets, and they clink softly in the silence. I slide the silver one on my wrist where it swings cold and heavy, laden with mementoes of her high school and college years: an etched calendar marked with her birthday, a miniature champagne bucket with the bottle tilting out, a medallion engraved with the name of her best friend, *Phyllis*. The other bracelet is gold with only a few charms, a bracelet left unfinished, waiting for more memories.

He is the only remaining emerald of the year. Though his jet horn and zig-zag legs are coated with dust from crawling along the ranch road, the shield behind his head glitters gold and copper, burnished just as bright as the rest of his split green armor. When I pick him up, he sends his puff-ball eyes out on the ends of their stalks—a June bug in November.

The hum of June beetles' wings was the sound of silence in the summer-time orchard of my childhood. They lit on the apricots, peaches, and plums, burrowing beneath the skins to sup and suck, and then dropped down to lay their eggs in the leaf mold and fruit rot. We caught the ancient-looking, hard-shelled creatures and flew them like kites from the ends of spools of sewing thread.

Today, this June beetle is too cold to open his jeweled case and fly away on thrumming black wings. He burrows in my jacket pocket. Back at the house, Lily makes him a nest in a box of dried rose petals and oak leaves that have crisped and fallen.

———•—•—

I am drawn downward, down off of the table-flat land where the grasses are dry and monotonous in winter, down as the water runs, down into the deep crack that carries it off to the river. I slide and slip on dry dirt and cured grasses, grasping at wild grapevine and stubbornly rooted broom weed until I reach the layer of the earth where the rainwater has carried away the soil. Stone steps and basins sit cold in the shade of the deep gully, the debris of fall and winter in their hollows, waiting for spring rains to carry it away. As I walk down the draw, the going gets easier and wider. My feet crunch and rustle through the dry vegetation as the walls of the prairie rise up around me.

He is only a flash, grayellow, on the edge of my vision. I hear him run-ning after I see him leave. I turn and clamber up the wall of the draw to the south-facing shelf where he was taking his nap. The grass is packed down in an oblong hollow. The ground is warm to the palm of my hand. The coyote is long gone.

The morning is made for webs, each strand highlighted by strings of drop-lets that mirror the world a million times over. She signs her web with a messy zigzag that mimics the markings on the underside of her belly. When it gets damaged by wind or a meal, she has a seemingly endless supply of strong floss within. She weaves because she must. She does her job and retires to the side, eating only that which stumbles into the filigree. She does the best job, chooses the best location, and sometimes takes a chance, attach-ing her line across a human's path or to a wheel that moves in the morning. And so she will begin again, swooping across the diameter, weaving and spinning for joy, for food—and for the hope of morning dew.

My son is set in gold. He rides a horse named Bananas, and the dirt kicked up in the big round pen shimmers in the morning air. Oscar and the colt move 'round and 'round and 'round, loping circles and figure eights. He reins to a stop, pats the colt's neck, and coaxes Bananas to take a few steps backward. He circles to the right, then circles to the left, teaching the colt to give to pressure. He talks to the little horse nonstop as he drops the hondo of his rope and lets it drag behind. They trot and then lope. Oscar dismounts to find a good-sized mesquite branch, ties it to his rope, and climbs back on. He pats and soothes and eases the colt into a walk, dragging the limb through the dirt. I hold my breath as he coils his rope, bringing the limb closer and closer, and finally up into his lap, bumping the colt's shoulder in the process. The colt stands, trusting, as the boy disentangles the stick and tosses it to the ground, lesson learned. They lope a few more circles before heading to the barn.

This is the second colt that my son has ridden this Sunday morning. The first one was silver.

Bling

Everything in this booth at the trade show shines: rings, bracelets, necklaces of heavy turquoise, cell phone cases, FatBaby boots in neon ostrich, jeans with rips in the knees and rhinestones on the hip pockets. Kippy belts are laid out flat on black velvet, row after row of shine.

Lily runs her fingers along the table, her stubby nails flecked with peeling-off polish, cuticles ragged from climbing on the hay stack. Her hair is caught back in a fuzzy ponytail. She has chocolate on her chin. She lifts one bright piece of costume jewelry after another, trying them on her thin wrists and holding them against her ten-year-old chest.

We leave the trade show carrying nothing but some goat's milk soap in a cotton bag.

———•—•———

The whole world is black velvet and scented with mesquite smoke. Diamonds glitter above us, jewels that by rights should never be obliterated except by storm clouds when the land is dry. They dance in the velvet regardless of our regard. At our feet are rubies laced with amber and citrine. Their intensity simmers and flares when the wind blows, and we feel their heat on our faces. We've eaten the salad, the potatoes, the steaks. We've seen the gift star as it streaked from horizon to horizon. And now the soggy-bottomed clouds that wrap around to the east melt the velvet with each silent flicker. When he hangs the lantern in the range tipi, our world narrows to that one glowing pyramid.

———•—•———

The wind is blowing fiercely on the warming side of solstice. Burn warnings are in effect. I wonder if Frost ever came to the Great Plains to see this gold that does stay, day after day.

There are whitecaps on the playa lake. The strip of dry land out in the middle that is usually teeming with egrets, geese, mallards, and pintails is bare except for a bald eagle who dines alone, picking at the remains of his breakfast. I didn't bring my camera, but it doesn't matter. I will be here again, where the coyote naps, the eagle feasts, June bugs stay until November, and the coals burn bright in the night.

Connie

She offered me a white bread sandwich layered with square ham and neon orange artificial cheese-food. Miracle Whip oozed from between the layers. When I declined, she ate three, chasing them with cheese puffs, not neon orange, but dusty, fingerprint powder orange. The kitchen was noisy and whirling. The door slammed open and closed, open and closed, the flies coming in as the cool air went out. The room rang with the voices of her children vying for attention, for food, to be heard. As always, she used one voice, the beautiful one, to address me, and another voice—strident, common, harsh—to address the children. They talked over the top of her and banged chairs and cabinets as she handed out sandwiches, each plastic bag with a child's name in black marker.

We have been friends for a decade, through births, afternoons at the creek, ranch rodeos in July, Wednesday night potluck suppers, job changes, and long periods of silence. I've cleaned her house and taught her children. I've sat with her in an ICU waiting room until we knew that her twenty-year-old foster son would survive the injuries sustained in a ranch wreck. We've slept in the same bed, gone on road trips together. Since I have known her she's owned and operated a day care, sold products in a pyramid scheme, and tried to stay home. Now she drives the fastest school bus in the district and teaches the children no one else wants in their classroom, fighting their battles and challenging them when they are lazy. Her hug is like a pillow, and she never lets go first.

She is always on a quest of some sort—for a better diet, a better car, a better housekeeper, a better job, a new product to make her life easier, more tools, more money, more fun, more reasons not to sit down, not to stay home, not to take a survey of her life, not to cry. She buys books she never reads, exercise equipment she never uses, ranch land in Oklahoma, clothes for all weights. Her schedule rivals that of a head of state; she's perpetually running late and always tired.

One spring she gave me a tour of her newly planted garden, the plowed earth fragrant, wooden stakes neatly labeling each row. A lawn chair was strategically placed beneath a small tree, and she told me of her plan to sit there each morning while she watered her plants, a peaceful slice of time to begin each day. Later in the summer, I saw her garden again, wild and dry, fence-high careless weeds, the lawn chair collapsed beneath the tree, goathead vines wound 'round its webbing. One lonely purple cabbage grew beside an uprooted stake with the faded word *peppers* written on it in black marker.

Nine years ago, I walked through a display of her art, watercolors and pastels of amazing depth and color. She hasn't painted since that exhibition because it didn't make any money. This summer, her daughter found a box of pastels among my craft supplies; she had never seen pastels before.

No matter what her bathroom scale says, her husband thinks she is beautiful. She speaks of him with exasperation, but I have seen her touch his face when he is tired. Like the number of broken cars in their driveway, the number of children living in their home fluctuates. Right now, she is cleaning up after five lunches, but two of her foster children are not with her. Being a ranch wife means too many miles of dirt road, not enough pay, and a

Connie

husband who can't always go to church with her. She reads romance novels with bare-chested cowboys on the covers, but only when she is on vacation.

Today she touches the cover of the book I am reading and laughs. "How in the world do you have time to read something like that?" She breathes like a faltering swimmer as she moves down the sidewalk, taking the noise level, the chaos, the futility-flavored urgency with her when she goes.

Frankie

He offered us a song about riding the eternal range, his mouth a wide gri-mace of pain, but his voice true to every note. His fiddle sang a song mim-icking a longhorn bull's bellow and danced through a song about a horse no one could ride. He listened to us with one hand cupped around his ear, a wide smile, and all of his attention. Just as his camp is nestled in the Canadi-an River prairie country, so he lives, nestled among the memorabilia of a life lived with the land and with his music. He invited us to sit and stay awhile in a room full of cigarette smoke and stories and songs, each illustrated with the wave or scrape of his bow.

His fiddle says what words cannot. We heard songs he wrote while sitting on the porch looking out over Camp Creek, songs he learned on the JA wagon when it stayed out for months at a time, and stories of people, horses, and ranches that no longer exist. We listened to music that arthritis cannot mar and technique cannot duplicate because it is rooted in a lifetime of art. We heard lyrics to "Good-bye Ol' Paint" that we had never heard before.

In the late evening, he invites us to walk out to his saddle house, a shrine to the days when he rode the prairie and a few thousand rough horses. He leans close to us as his stories take him back to a time when he moved with more surety and his bones did not ache. "A horse can only think of one thing at a time." The swollen, knotted wrists move in a practiced gesture, distracting an ornery company horse that is trying to make his yesterday mornings interesting. Old-time methods and wisdom spill from him like jewels, and we scoop up all that we can.

We stand with our backs to the evening sun watching two old horses graze and stomp at flies, as much in retirement as the man who feeds them each morning. He looks out over the prairie and tells us that he is moving to town. He is bothered by the fact that he lives here, taking up one of the camps on a big working cow outfit when his stirrups are crisscrossed with cobwebs and his headstalls are brittle with age. This old cowboy's sense of place is strong, though he doesn't own this short-grass country that encourages a man to love, to survive, to know, a land that nurtures abilities unappreciated in the modern world. He tells us that he doesn't want to impose on these kind people any longer, but his voice breaks, and he turns his head away. He'll put off the move as long as possible so that maybe it won't be necessary.

As the sun sets, he will play his fiddle and look over the cottonwoods of Camp Creek.

Cloud Come to Earth

We are under a winter storm advisory, but I can't find the storm. There is no thunder, no lightning, no boiling, roiling clouds. No navy-blue norther, no blizzard, no knife-edged winds. A thick heavy blanket of moisture and arctic air sits low over the land, obscuring what is usually an immense bowl of prairie and sky, substituting instead insubstantial cottony curtains that shift and change and hover.

The house is a hot stew of chaos. Oscar scrambles eggs along with chorizo and bangs cabinet doors looking for the cheese shredder. Lily sings a Christmas song along with Reba, and the tree lights blink. The dogs whine to go in and out, in and out, hesitating to put paws on burning cold concrete. Nick hunts for the phone, hunts for the phone book, hunts for some paper, drinks the dregs from the coffeepot. And I look out of the windows.

I put on two pair of socks, thermal underwear, jeans, sweatshirt, crocheted cap and scarf, tennis shoes, fleece jacket, lined ski gloves, and another fleece with a hood. I struggle with the zippers because I should have put the gloves on last. My world is framed by the cap and hood. My shoes grapple for traction on the frozen rocks and dirt of the ranch road as I walk like a toddler to the grassy edge, arms slightly away from my sides, each step careful and deliberate. The dogs' coats are immediately flecked with white, and their feet scrabble in the slick wheel ruts. Walking on the icy grass is less precarious, but each step crunches loudly in the foggy air.

A week ago the prairie was yellow-brown and in constant motion. The grasses shivered, waved, and rolled. The air around the playa lake resounded with the calls of Canada geese, pintails, widgeon, mallards, snow geese, and herons. The water danced in peaks and ripples.

Today the land is motionless and silent. Each blade of grass glistens thickly, standing with head bent, fragile. The yellow landscape is heavily overlaid with whites, grays, blues, and black. The broom weed is a caricature of itself, the details blurred, each element of form magnified and made ponderous by ice. The playa is solid and still. Icy moisture drifts straight downward, not rain, not snow, not sleet, just cloud come to earth.

On the back side of the pasture I stop the loud crunch, crunch, crunch of my feet. Silence. I shake back my hood and pull off my cap. I can hear the dogs breathing.

If I wore infrared goggles I could find the birds. I could find the ground squirrels, the cottontails, the coons, the porcupines, the foxes in their dens. I could find the field mice all curled up in their beds. The goggles would show me where the antelope spend icy days, where the owls sleep. They would show a huge hot red glow where the house stands with lights on and kettle steaming. Where beans simmer on the stove with garlic and onion and the kids wrap gifts behind closed bedroom doors. Where cookie dough chills in the freezer. Where the chickens complain and fuss and stay on their roosts with their feet tucked up under their breast feathers. Where the horses sleep under the barn, hips cocked and fragrant breath visible. Where the dogs will nap on the couch when we get home.

A hawk flies from tree to tree in the creek. At the northernmost point in my hike, I come across some ghostly steers who chew popsicle grass and raise their heads to gaze at me through the damp. Only my thighs and my cheeks are cold. I wish I could pound tipi stakes into the frozen ground, gather my wool blankets, and cut enough mesquite wood to last the day. I'd curl up in the woodsmoke and wool, wrap my tail around my nose like a coyote, and watch this cloud come to earth.

Used To

The bay horse grunted out of habit more than indignation as the kid pulled the girth tight out of habit more than necessity. The young man looked around, uncertain, bridle over one arm, halter rope draped over the other. Damp wind blew out of the east, ruffling the kid's hair between his hat and the starched collar of his clean white western shirt. With a bent head and a reluctance that rarely marked his demeanor when getting ready to ride, he slid the headstall of his bridle over the horse's ears and carefully laid the halter in the back of the pickup. He watched the men around him before stepping into a pair of work-worn and blood-stained leggings that had seen more branding pens than the kid had. Only when the slowly growing group of quiet men on their horses had grown to a sizeable number did he suck his hat down and swing into the saddle.

Nick and Ricky Bud leaned against a white Ford Explorer parked in the middle of the street and watched the whole process, not out of interest or curiosity so much as dullness and numbness. Ricky Bud had lit a cigarette as he came down the steps of the high school auditorium above, the biggest building in the community. It was still not big enough to hold all of the people who had parked their cars and pickups along the highway, filled up the asphalt lots around the school, and spilled over onto the dirt lot beside the roping arena down below. He bowed his head reverently each time he brought the cigarette to his lips.

Men were saddling horses all around them, but the air was flat and somber, only the stomp of horses and slap of leather to break the silence. The only smile to be seen was on the face of a small girl standing beside her mother, offering a handful of rocks gathered like treasure from the ground. Her mother tried to smile back at her, but it was a broken fraction of her normal expression. A battered wooden wagon, painted red at one time and hitched to a pair of sleeping mules, sat at the head of the line of cars that blocked the street. An hour before, a weeping mother, stony-faced father, and bewildered younger brother had stumbled from the first car and into the auditorium. Now a receiving line snaked in one door and out the other. The people coming out looked deflated and undone.

The group of mounted men grew. While some faces wore deep lines and the sharp eyes of experience, most of them were smooth-shaven, lean, and raw. So many times over the last few years this same group has gathered in ever-changing combinations and numbers at ranch rodeos, branding pens, trading parties, dances, and parking lots, a blend of rowdy confidence and youthful shyness, taking their hats off to shake a lady's hand, spitting in the dirt, and breathing the air of possibility. This past July, those with enough natural ability, bravado, and cash carried their saddles, balancing them on one hip, stopping often to shake hands with friends on the way to the crow's nest to sign the waiver, count out the bills, and draw a bronc for the show. Surrounded by friends and advice, each one hunched his shoulders, sat back on his tailbone, and nodded his head, unfolding on the first solid jump to ride tall, straight, leaning back on the bronc rein, victorious. When the judges turned in the final scores, they slapped the winner on the back and spent the rest of the night helping him celebrate, the shyness gone, the rowdiness real.

Today there is no winner. They've encountered death before, but never one of their own. Never one who represented all that is strong and good and handsome and athletic and fine. There is no sense to be made of a wrecked pickup on a dark two-lane road, taking away the life of one so young. So they sit on their gentlest horses with down-turned gazes as his girlfriend is half-carried down the steps. Three days hence someone will report that they saw her, just sitting beside the mound of fresh dirt, wearing his Carhartt coat.

Ricky Bud dropped the butt to the ground and snuffed it with his boot heel. Nick watched the bay horse walk by, and nodded his head. "I used to have those leggings." Ricky Bud fingered the red carnation in his buttonhole, dreading the task before him as he prepared to go back up the steps where he would shoulder one of the heaviest loads of his life and slide it into the back of the wagon to be drawn slowly up the dirt road to the windblown cemetery, followed by a silent procession of families in cars and mounted compadres who will show their respect the only way they know how. Then he sighed deeply and the lines in his face softened.

"There's lots of things we used to have around here."

Ten Inches of Sand

The season for shipping cattle is over. There isn't a cloven hoof on the ranch other than the deer and antelope that drink from the playa lakes and heel-fly ponds. Nick and Oscar have been discussing materials and measurements for months. Now the boy holds the end of the tape measure as they plant stakes in a circle nestled in the wedge of ground between the west horse pasture, the barn lots, and the hay shed, forty feet in diameter. The boy writes on the back of his leather glove, applying his algebra skills to the project. He is startled when he realizes that his dad has already done the figuring in his head.

Seven freshly weaned colts watch the activity from behind the barbed-wire fence, no longer leggy and cute, but awkward and clumsy, lonely and irritable without their mamas nearby.

Thirteen holes, three feet deep, to set eleven-foot posts made of two and three eighths inch pipe. Sweaty work for a boy who will be six feet tall a year from now.

On warm days, the round pen takes form. Hot work, even in November, unloading and shoving cross ties in place to form a barrier at the bottom of the circle to keep the sand from spilling out. Hot work, too, shoveling damp sand out of the bed of a pickup. Ten inches deep.

The welder chugs while Nick secures the top rail and sucker-rod bands. Boring work for the boy who mustn't look at the arc, standing for long minutes holding the heavy metal still and in place.

———•—•———

Cedar posts have been piled beside the hay shed for months, the outer bark flaking off in long strips, the chickens laying eggs in the empty spaces between.

Cattle trucks roll in from the Mexican border, dumping off fresh yearlings. The round pen stands, an unfinished skeleton, while the boy helps doctor sick cattle, prowling through them on horseback, learning to spot a drooping ear and fevered nose. He practices roping in the pasture, the whole process different outside of a branding pen or an arena and in the absence of a dummy with plastic horns. His hands are too full, and the action too fast. When he catches his first steer, he forgets to dally, and his rope goes trailing away while he sits empty-handed, frustrated and angry at his father for not letting him tie hard and fast until he is older, more experienced.

When the steers finally graze in the pastures, and the ones that died have been eaten by coyotes and the buzzards who returned with the spring, the boy carries every six-foot cedar post to his dad, who ties them firmly to the sucker-rod bands with stay wire. A gate of weathered gray wood waits, leaned up against the barn, salvaged from some falling-down pens, its heavy form ready to be put back into good use.

———•—•———

The colts' shaggy hair blows away with the spring winds. They have established a pecking order, the sorrel with the star between his eyes reigning over his half brothers. The boy turns the pages of his algebra book, each day bringing him closer to the back cover. The warm air blowing in the windows makes it hard to concentrate on variables and exponents. His mind is on a circle, and ten inches of fresh sand.

Bésame

The round pen is a golden bowl of sand, sky, and cedar posts in the early spring sun. My fleece jacket and sweatshirt lie across a hay bale outside the gate. My tools—buggy whip, lariat rope, leather gloves, halter, cotton lead rope—lie in the center of the circle. The third colt of the day stirs up dust in the alley as he runs by me twice before I get him cut away from the wad of yearlings and into our classroom. As I swing the heavy gate closed and wrestle with the chain, he trots back and forth on the opposite side of the round pen, head held high, looking for a way back to the comfort of the group.

He was conceived on the prairie and born during a cold, wind-swept spring night one year ago, unimprinted, uncoddled. His registered name is Kiss Me Cowboy, offspring of Luckys Jo Jo and My Precious Cowgirl. He spent the first few months of his life as part of a mob made up of stud, mares, and other foals on the watershed of the Salt Fork of the Red River. When we weaned this batch of colts, he was the first one to touch me with his nose, kiss me in greeting. I call him Bésame.

When I walk to the center of the pen and turn my back on him, deciding which tools to use for this, his third lesson, I feel him take two steps in my direction. I can almost smell his shaggy winter hair that he won't need much longer. I choose the buggy whip and position myself to move toward his rear. He stamps his front feet nervously before he moves out, away from me, plowing the deep sand with each step. The round pen grows warmer as we utilize its shape, 'round and 'round and 'round. When I cut off his path, he stops and faces me dead-on. He offers me his head, a sign of understanding from the previous two sessions. His relief is always in submission.

He stands his ground as I walk up and put my fingertips on his neck, giving him the comfort of a scratch, a pat, a rub. As the session progresses, I move with less care, making my motions bigger, offering him the knowledge that no matter how big they become, no matter where I touch him, no matter how vigorously I scratch or how loud a pat resounds, it doesn't hurt. I introduce the halter slowly, and he steps like a marionette, marching toward me to find relief from my tugs on the cotton lead rope. Even in submission he is proud, his posture stiff.

———•———

Early last spring, I sat on the pipe fence of the corral and watched while two untouched two-year-olds were unloaded from the trailer. A friend of mine from Germany picked the bright red roan and I picked the darker one, my very first attempt at doing the ground work with a colt. We spent a week in side-by-side square pens as we practiced the methods that we discussed for hours at the kitchen table, warming cold hands on enamel coffee mugs. By the end of the week, in triumph, we were able to halter, lead, and groom our respective colts, even picking up their feet. They went from running wild, scared, self-destructive circles around us to gentled, almost pets. She named hers Nudel, and I named mine Trusty.

Trusty and I learned our lessons together. I stepped on his toes, and he stepped on mine. I made mistakes and accidentally taught them to him. He taught me some lessons in safety. I taught him some lessons in manners.

———•———

I quit tugging on the lead rope and move into Bésame's personal space.

Bésame

Surrounded by the smell of damp sand, damp horse, and the palest green grass of the year, I lay my hands on his warm shoulder, the day's benediction, praise for a job well done, a moment of grace. He kisses me in more sweetness than any lover has ever done by leaning his head between my breasts, by overcoming his instinct to flee. He lets out a long sigh, the tension of learning new things released in the embrace. Silent and still, partners, Bésame and I, in a classic dance of give and take, lovers holding and letting go, one species blessed by another, friends relaxed and in tune, here in the round pen.

The Round Pen

Oscar won't shut up in the house, but we can't get him to talk to his horses out at the barn. Algebra is his nemesis, but numbers are important to him. He'll tell you that he is almost fourteen, that he is starting a couple of two-year-old colts this summer, and that he is leaving home when he is eighteen. Exactly one year ago, he sat in the saddle house sobbing in frustration because we were holding him back, prohibiting him from spending the $75 entry fee for the Open Ranch Bronc Riding at the Clarendon Fourth of July celebration.

Today he is fidgeting around, standing taller with bravado as he gets ready to ride these colts for the first time. His voice deepens as he tells me that Shiney has been being a brat in their ground sessions, and that he pitched with the saddle the other day. Oscar observes that perhaps the little horse just isn't ready to be ridden. I've been running interference between this boy, who is so much like me, and his dad for two years now, ever since his voice broke and lowered an octave.

The colts are roan bookends. Shiney is blue, and Presidente is red. I know them as well, or better, than I know my son. They are easier to get to know and don't change on me overnight.

I stop to rub Shiney where he stands tied to the fence, and he walks all over me, easygoing and too gentle. He gets in my personal space and bumps me with his nose, asking to be scratched on the sweet spot under his belly. He's been known to nip at me when I don't give him enough attention. He's a brat sometimes, and he lacks confidence, which makes him sull up when pushed.

Presidente tosses his head and does a token side step when I walk up. His hot blood gives him the confidence that Shiney lacks, and he stands with a cocky, alert air. He gets angry easily, but is quick to forgive and eager to learn new things. I have been working with these colts for over a year, doing all of the groundwork possible so that this first ride will be easier.

Nick has been putting off this day for weeks. He looks tired and almost bored as he helps Oscar put a bit in Presidente's mouth, but his voice snaps impatiently when the headstall is too big for the colt, and he must punch a new hole in the leather.

Even in the early evening the round pen is a bowl of heat except for a pool of shade on the west side. I stand at the gate, stooping slightly to peer between the slats. The sun is opposite me, throwing the men I love into relief and glinting off the silver and leather on Presidente's back. Prez stands with hip cocked and blinks his eyes sleepily as Oscar tightens the girth. Nick sends the colt away in a big circle, and he trots around under the saddle, loose and easy, a wondering look in his eye. He goes the other way just as easily, calm and moving smoothly. When Nick tells him to whoa, he turns and faces and steps slowly toward the men.

Oscar grabs a stirrup and slaps it down hard to see how the colt will react. Nick growls, "Get ahold of that son of a bitch! Are you going to have to get kicked before you remember?" The boy gathers the reins up high on the colt's neck, getting a good grip on him so he can't run by and kick if he is startled. When Oscar is ready to mount, Nick walks up to the colt's head and grasps the reins close to the bit. His last instructions are a quiet murmur while the boy nods his head before pulling his jeans up and sucking his hat down.

Nick pulls his own hat down and hitches up his own Levi's, his whole body focused and tense.

Too soon, Oscar is in the saddle. There is a long moment of absolute stillness as Presidente absorbs the new position of the boy, and the man stands ready to help him if the colt loses his mind. Nothing happens, and Nick steps aside to let the colt move out.

Awkward under the unaccustomed weight, the colt puts his feet down carefully in the deep sand, but soon he is trotting the circumference, looking smug at the new lesson he seems to have mastered easily. Oscar laughs and makes a joke, his hands relaxed on the reins in his relief that the colt isn't going to pitch, but Nick barks an order that makes him get his mind back in the middle.

While the men switch the saddle and bridle to Shiney, I treat Presidente to a cool bath with the water hose. The lowering sun turns the water to crystal. The red horse preens under the cold spray, turns to burgundy, and drinks out of the hose.

Shiney moves stiffly and sulls up from time to time, but the session still goes so well that we laugh in relief at our fears. Nick sits on the barn steps and drinks a beer while I spray Shiney down. Oscar chatters nonstop.

As we walk to the house, Nick's arm is heavy on my shoulder.

Next day, the earth has come full circle, and the evening sun reflects off of a million particles of dust as the same cast graces the round corral stage once more.

"Talk to him, son! Talk to that pony!"

"About what?" The boy's voice is strident with frustration, tight and resistant, not wanting to repeat the words we offer him but not coming up with any of his own.

"It doesn't matter! Just talk! Let him know you are up there. Girls! Talk to him about girls!"

The boy laughs, his anger melted by the little bit of humor. He leans down to pat the blue colt, and his body jerks when Shiney moves out quickly, startled by the change in shadow and pressure. Shiney trots around the round pen, more relaxed today. They get him up into a lope on the second circle, and the session ends on a successful note. Oscar switches horses, and I shield my eyes from the sun once more as they begin Presidente's second lesson.

"It's ok, Prez. Same thing as yesterday. You're ok." The boy reaches for words to murmur, forgetting to say whoa when the colt ambles to a stop. Nick talks to Oscar about sitting tight while he gets Prez to move out again. The first circle goes fast. Prez breaks into a lope, throwing his head up, his eyes wide and his tail clamped too tight as he plows the deep sand around the edges of the pen. Nick halts the process and spends some time helping Oscar calm the nervous colt.

When they make him move out again, in the opposite direction, the little horse gives in to his fear. His eyes are wild, and he bogs his head after he breaks into a lope. I can't see very much other than the inverted U that is my colt, the batlike shape up above him that is my son, and the uncaring sun behind them both. I hear the whump as Oscar hits hard. The rest is a shining blur of sand, squeals, and my son's huge eyes as he fights to get out of the gate, out of the scared colt's path. Sand showers into my hair and the collar of my shirt as I hold Oscar up while his paralyzed diaphragm recovers from the fall, and he finally gulps in air. The angry father uses a lariat rope to show the colt's rear how unprofitable pitching can be. The boy recovers and shakes me off, impatient with my hovering, and, inside the round pen, the colt slows to a halt.

As the sand settles back to earth, the four of us convene inside the pen, six trembling hands, four pounding hearts, and one very shaken grown man. When Oscar begins to berate himself for not sticking with the colt, the big man explodes, poking him in the chest and telling him to "get over your bad self!" The explosion is one big flash, over quickly. The man squats at the edge of the shade, leaning against the cedar stays, while the boy, in tears, and the shamefaced little horse retreat to the other side of the pen, leaving me in the middle.

I want to go sit beside Nick, but instead I must reassure my son that his perfectionist tendencies are honest, born into his makeup, genetic from both sides of the blanket. The peacemaking doesn't take very long as the fear that spurred the anger subsides. Soon, Nick stands up and walks to a spot to the right of the wooden gate. He uses the heel of his boot to draw a large crescent in the sand. He turns, grinning.

"There, son. You own a piece of this round pen."

The Address Book

He reads aloud, beginning with entries that start with *A* while I fill the kitchen sink with hot, soapy water. The leather cover of his address book is curled, creased, and worn smooth. It fits his hands. The kitchen is the warmest room in the house as the coffeemaker finishes dripping a fresh pot.

Nick and Oscar left horseback a few minutes ago, their breath a frosty trail. Lily bundled up to go check on her hideouts before her cousins arrive. My grandfather frets that it is too cold for her out there and moves his hands in meaningless gestures as I begin clearing away the breakfast dishes. So . . . he reads each name, the mailing address, the zip code, the phone number.

He shows me where he crossed out my own address many times as we moved from ranch to ranch through the years. He remembers visiting me at each one, driving over rough dirt roads, following instructions written in his notebook. He drove down into the Palo Duro Canyon one winter, ahead of a blue norther that dumped several inches of snow over the mesquites and cedars and slick red roads.

"Don't you remember, Nita?" My grandfather bellowed at my grandmother as if she were hard of hearing. The light coming through the kitchen window was dim as more snow floated out of gray skies.

"Our first grandchild born in a hospital way up there in Spearman where Tom was working in that feedlot! But they closed the roads, and we had to spend the night in Amarillo! Found a hotel and had to stay the night. Snow everywhere. And that was in April!" He wanted her to remember so he just kept talking. The coffeepot was empty, as were her eyes.

He bundled up in layers to go out with Nick to feed cattle. They dragged a tire behind the feed pickup, making a path through the snow to the dry grass below so the cattle could find the cake they dumped along the trail. He came back more rested than he had been in weeks.

I stayed behind with the children and my grandmother, feeding the wood-burning stove with sticks of mesquite to keep her warm. She paced from window to door to window, declaring that she was *not* going out in the snow and that I could *not* make her. I pried her fingers from the handle of a knife she found in the kitchen. I pleaded with her not to take off her clothes in the living room. I held her when she cried like a child because she couldn't find him, the one person she still recognized.

—————•—•—————

I clear butter, jellies, and leftover bacon from the table. He reads me the address of the Alzheimer's Association before he turns the page. As he reads along through surnames beginning with *B* through *D,* he comments on each entry. This one is an old employee who used to drive a tractor for him in the alfalfa fields. Now he lives in Albany and has sixteen grandchildren.

—————•—•—————

I spent a week with them every summer when I was a little girl. Every day I rode to the farm with my grandfather while my grandmother worked at the bank in town. Each day at noon he took me to a different restaurant. I always ordered a salad and a baked potato unless we went to Rosa's Cocina or the China Kitchen. He didn't like for me to leave food on my plate.

Back out at the farm in the afternoons, I stripped to my panties, leaving my clothes on the hot blue pickup seat, and tiptoed over rocks and dirt to the concrete verge of the irrigation ditch. He would lean over the motor until it chugged to life. After a few roaring moments when it looked as if nothing was going to happen, a white head of water rushed out of the pipe and swept down the ditch carrying dirt and debris ahead of it as far as I could see. When the first rush was over and the water flowed clear, I caught his eye in the deafening roar. After he nodded his head, I eased off into the stream. The flow carried me as he walked alongside, setting the magic black straws that spilled water over his dry West Texas fields, cupping his palm over the ends and giving one strong motion to set the water flowing. I tried swimming upstream when I got ahead of him, but eventually just floated along until I reached the end of the field where I caught the handle of the sluice gate, pulled myself out, and lay on the hot apron until he caught up, his face and arms almost blackened by the sun.

He bought me my first bottle of sunscreen after the doctors cut the cancers off of his face.

———•—•———

The *H* pages of his address book are full. He reads through the names of my siblings and parents. He pauses at the name of my paternal grandfather who died this past year at ninety-six years old. These two old men lived in the same town, attended the same First Baptist Church, shared four grandchildren, but always seemed as if they were from two different worlds.

He can't bear to come for the holidays empty-handed, so the UPS man delivered four big boxes from Swiss Colony earlier in the week. He called from Plainview to get my last-minute grocery list, but refused to go to Walmart because "they don't let those people say Merry Christmas anymore." Soon the house will swarm with great-grandchildren. Some of them will sleep in the motor home with him while the Panhandle winds rock it from side to side.

I scrape dried egg off the stove, wipe out the microwave, and pour him a fresh cup of coffee while he reads through *M*—the names of my cousins, my uncle, the name of the woman my uncle married on the patio of my grandparents' home.

———•—•———

The lights of the hospital room were dim. The halls were silent. The hard plastic chairs made my tailbone ache until we found some flat pillows for padding. My aunt and I held hands across my grandmother's frail body all night long, hearing each breath as it came and went. She isn't married to my mother's brother anymore, but that doesn't make her any less my aunt.

I was only three years old at her wedding. My sister was an infant, and my mother's full breasts strained the bodice of her blue gown. I was older when they got a divorce, already married myself.

I noticed, that night, that though we are not related by blood, our hands are the same size.

———•—•———

I load the dishwasher while he reads through the names of war buddies and college roommates who have died or are dying. He goes to a lot of funerals. The names of cousins, twice removed. One of them just got married for the first time in her late thirties. One of them runs a children's bookstore in California. One owns a bar in Austin. He reads the name of my grandmother's doctor, the one who fixed her jaw when she fell and broke it on the concrete.

I wipe the red and green tablecloth, carefully picking up the photographs of her grave that he has brought to show the family when they all arrive, laden with packages and food. The family plot is brilliantly green in the brown desert cemetery. He offers me the only bit of poetry I have ever heard him speak as he tells me about the deer that fly over the stone walls each morning to graze on my grandmother's well-watered plot.

He tells me about his trip to New York City to visit his newest great-grandchild, about the cab driver whose brother lives in El Paso, about riding the subway, about flying on my uncle's frequent-flyer miles. "Because he gets those flyer miles from his company, I flew round-trip for only $219! Two hundred and nineteen dollars." He shakes his head and turns the page.

He reads the names of business associates who are no longer in business, luncheon partners who live in assisted-living facilities, the name of his heart doctor, and the name of the county commissioner who took his place when he decided not to run again. He still goes to his office at 804 North Main Street most days and takes naps on the couch through the long afternoons. He got a traffic ticket this month for not wearing his seat belt between his office and the bank, three blocks he has driven almost every day of his life.

He reads the name of my mother's cousin whose wife died this fall. At the funeral luncheon, he handed me his pen and a napkin and asked me to write a list of every person in the room who was related to him. When I finished the list, checking it twice like a conscientious first child, he looked it over and scoffed, doubting that I had gotten an accurate count. Surely there are more people who will come to his own funeral.

The kitchen is clean, the floor swept, and preparations made for lunch by the time he reads the last zip code, mispronouncing the Spanish surname of the maid who hurt her back while caring for my grandmother in her last days.

————•—•——

The morning is warm for late December. The trash barrel is smoking, boxes and wrapping paper turned to ashes. The smell of Windex still hangs in the air. Moments ago, my grandfather stood beside me giving the windshield of his motor home a brisk polish, pointing out the ding that turned into a spreading crack. "Truck," he barked gruffly.

I shade my eyes to watch the motor home turn like a big cumbersome bug onto the pavement at the end of the lane. He's never been very good at good-byes. He tried to engineer this one by taking all morning to unplug his house on wheels and make it secure for the long journey back to the big, empty, white house on 7D Road, four hundred miles to the south.

At last he slammed the driver's side door with a curt, "I'm going."

A Legacy of Snakes and Stones

He walks over the desert amidst greasewood and roadrunners. He walks over rocky mountains. He walks over river breaks amidst cedars and feral hogs. He walks over short-grass flats under wheeling kites. He walks in spring when the dirty wind blows him sideways, in summer when evening mosquitoes worry his ears, in fall when the air smells laden and tired, in winter when enduring the chill is justifiable payment for being out of doors. He walks in spite of her phone calls to the children.

Your dad is having a hard time again. My mother's words are familial code warning us of a return of the suffocating depression that envelops him from time to time, that swamps his life in waves. *He's spending a lot of time driving out into the country.* Not much more will be said. We all know that she sits at home and worries while he is gone for hours, out walking over the land.

When he finishes walking, he sits, sometimes for whole afternoons. He stops moving, seeking a perfect stillness. The land becomes his private cinema, letting its shows both soothe and stoke the passion that has fueled his walking. Later he is driven to search library shelves for the intimate biographies of ants, for the names of the rocks, the birds, the weeds, the grasses. Often he is drawn back to some treasure day after day: to watch nests of Mississippi kites and Mexican eagles, immersed in the brief childhoods of the hatchlings, to sit for long hours, close to a coyote den, watching the pups tumble and growl and nurse through the warm afternoon.

One such day, when he had finished walking, he and a cottontail sat alone in a desert draw, framed by sun, silence, and sand. The air smelled damp with submoisture saved up during the wet spring. The cottontail grazed on the tender new green shoots carpeting a sandbar. The sand threw the heat from the sun into the peaceful pocket as the afternoon passed.

He would never have told the story later—there would have been no story to tell—no action, no narrative—if there had been no snake, no stone.

The intrusion was gradual. The interruption was slow to dawn on his consciousness. The scene shifted from mundane and pacific to threatened and raw as a sensuous shape in the sand became a hungry head that rose and swayed, casting a diamond shadow as it focused on the unwary cottontail.

My father threw a stone. There where he had gone to sit, to stop moving. There where he sought nothing. He threw a stone, one he doesn't remember picking up. He hurled a stone that found its mark without thought or conscious aim. He found a stone—and threw it.

———•—•———

The contractions were evenly spaced, as if my body had a clock. The couch was both my enemy and my cradle, holding me as I writhed through each clenching interval. I had done this years before, in a darkened hospital room, my mother pacing the hall with her Bible in her hand, praying, and my husband sitting upright in an uncomfortable chair in the corner, napping. I lay there on my side, enduring with the hope of every woman for that pink and pale blue crowning moment when it would all be over. That experience ended happily, if not according to my expectations, with a cesarean section and a healthy baby boy. My daughter's birth was scheduled, less risky, skipping my role almost entirely.

This time, I had failed to ask the doctor all of the right questions. My books didn't cover the subject of delivering miscarriage and loss. This pregnancy was over before it got a chance to begin. Upon hearing the news, I had mistakenly thought that nature always knew the right course to take.

And so I had waited, driving to the lab each week to give blood, giving time a chance to take away the tissue and the hormones. When nothing definitive happened, I took home a small vial of white tablets, magic pills, chemicals to end the waiting and let me get on with my usual cycle of womanhood. The grief, after all, had been with me for some time.

The day had been short and dark, rain pouring from the sky, making mire out of the twelve-mile ribbon of red dirt that led to the pavement. The pills had brought this pain, this every five minutes seeking for delivery. The evening brought fear, for none of it seemed natural or right. We debated the passability of the roads, but after a staticky cell phone call, set out anyway, the doctor waiting for us in the emergency room eighty miles away. The windshield wipers and the bump and grind of the four-wheel drive through the thick, clinging mud made no impression on me as I alternately bent over in silent pain then straightened up to breathe and reassure the children in the backseat that "Momma is fine. I just need to see the doctor in Amarillo."

The headlights showed both standing water and falling water, shifting from side to side in the tortuous dig, squirming sideways as the back wheels came around, glistening mesquites instead of road, and now shining sheets of water where the wheel ruts should be, bright red mud on either border. When the bridge spanning the first creek came in sight, I begged my husband to stop on the grassy verge so I could step out into the rain.

I needed to walk. In the early stages of labor with my son, I had walked up and down the echoing, brightly lit halls of the hospital, holding someone's arm, excited and eager. This time I only walked a few steps in the rain-muffled dark, alone, bewildered and dreading. Moisture misted my hair and my shoes sank into the squishy soft land as I squatted there, smelling exhaust from the pickup mixed with wet loamy ground and salt cedars. I closed my eyes, resisting the idea of an antiseptic hospital room among strangers. I tilted my head back, wishing I could stay there in that drizzle, lie down in that thick natural mud, wrap myself and my pain in the cold draws of Mulberry Creek.

A Legacy of Snakes and Stones

As I squatted there, wishing, a mass of spongy tissue and fluid rushed from me, as if called by my wishing. Nick came around the side of the truck. Staying out of the beam of the headlights, we stared at the mass in my two cupped hands. Sensing his bewilderment, I attempted to explain. "It's the miscarriage. It is done." He glanced toward the two little heads in the cab of the truck and back at the mass. He took it from me and wordlessly threw it into the bushes at the side of the bridge, wiping his hands on his Levi's.

We slipped and slid home through the darkness and the continuing rain, a phone call to the doctor the only thing breaking the silence. I held my streaked hands, palms up, in my lap.

———•—•———

I am sitting on a stone—not a very comfortable stone, not a convenient stone, not even a warm stone. The prairie is sleepy and grouchy, inhospitable today. A cold wind that bites beneath hems and steals my ability to stand still and see sweeps around her curves. The tired sun, having given its hottest and best a month ago, is filtered by sly gray clouds that sport white cotton candy bouffant tops like old ladies just from the beauty parlor. It is fall; the prairie dons an end-of-year cloak just like the forests and mountains do. Hers is more subtle maybe, more subdued, like a matron who still enjoys dressing up in fine, rich fabrics but doesn't need to compete with the flamboyant young girls. The one frivolous adornment she won't give up is the whispering gold jewelry of the cottonwoods in the draws.

And it is that shade of gold that the painters back behind me are discussing.

An hour earlier, we all clambered out of the cluttered ranch pickup after bouncing over mounds of bear grass between the dirt road and this, my favorite high point on the ranch. All three of us reached immediately for the snaps and zippers on our jackets when the pickup doors slammed behind us. I stood, hands tucked into my coat pockets, while they walked over the point, this way and that, looking, framing the landscape in their minds.

He found his spot, that place where the view offered him something that doesn't translate into words and the ground wasn't too uneven. Methodically, he began to unpack the backpack and the wooden box, standing the easel up on its legs, working the thumbscrews and adjusting the height just right. Next he peered around, looking at the light, making a decision about which color paper he would use as a base for the first painting. After making a choice, he attached it, already cut to the exact size, with blue tape to the easel. He clipped a much-washed, now-clean white towel to the edge of the paint box, convenient for wiping his fingertips between colors. He unfolded a cunning little container and filled it with water from a bottle in his backpack, just in case he wants to do a wash of watercolor beneath the chalk. The lids of the box unfolded to reveal the colors, lined up neatly in graduated rows, no greens mixed with the reds, no yellows amidst the browns.

She is a doctoral student, her days spent studying scientific theory, her funds going to food and rent. She has a plain easel, one she didn't even bother to set completely up, leaving the legs all different lengths, a sideways spider, because she was exclaiming over the colors heralding a sunset two hours away. She grabbed a box of pastels and slid it open to reveal a jumble of chalk pieces, all different sizes and brands. She dug in her backpack for a pad of paper and three pieces slid out onto the ground to be blown about by the wind.

He uses a pencil to lightly sketch in the feminine contours of the landscape that lies before him, reducing the sage and saffron and sandy browns to faint black lines on mauve paper. He stands braced against the cold wind, intent on each fine stroke of his pencil, each fine line, each fine detail of color when he finally picks among them with a long, pointing index finger, choosing, discarding, choosing, testing, murmuring to himself.

She has almost finished her first painting. There are pastels sown over the ground like rainbow bird droppings. Her hands are washed with chalky colors that match the streaks on her jeans. There is a smear of violet on her cheek, making her look like a part of the sky. She runs from one place to another, a clutch of pastels in her hand, using her knees for a place to rest her paper, sometimes even using the bumpy ground as an easel. She exclaims delightedly each time she finds the perfect color to sweep across the page, layering the paints on heavy and thick and bright. Soon she abandons one sheet of paper, placing it haphazardly under the edge of her backpack to rustle in the wind while she begins sweeping color on a new sheet, turning to face the west where all of the more vivid hues and shades of the day are gathering, blending, melting. Now she has a smudge of green on the tip of her nose. Turning suddenly, she grabs up a piece of stray paper and thrusts it at me along with a handful of chalk. I accept her offering and walk over to the stone.

He steps back from his work over and over again. His long-fingered musician's hands hold the paints steady, and he uses very small strokes, subtle, fine, precise. Each of his paintings is the size of a loaf pan, easy to frame, offering the perfect study from three steps back.

She paints on whatever size paper is available, and holds it at arm's length lest it blow away in the wind. She uses her stubby fingers to smear and blend. The paper is flamboyant with color in the center, fading to fingerprint-smudged white along the edges. One of her paintings has a crescent-shaped indention on one edge where she held it in her teeth while scrabbling around in the box for the fragment of ochre that she knew had to be in there somewhere.

The talk of value and shade back behind me doesn't make sense as I attempt to put the bitchy prairie on paper. And she *is* bitchy today. Tired of summer, tired of being nice, tired of sustaining life. It is time for her to nap, to rest, to go dormant. The cold wind rattles our papers, turns the little container of water into a splashing pendulum, and scuttles a cloud across the sun, changing the light drastically before anyone has a chance to get it all down on paper.

The cold of my stone seat has seeped up through my clothes, through my skin, through my flesh, until it has become a part of my bones. Or maybe the warmth of my bones has crept downward into the stone. I don't know where I end and where the granite begins.

Two bottles of red wine await us on the kitchen table at home. We'll pull out our paintings and prop them on the kitchen cabinet. They will kindly compliment some small element of mine while roundly criticizing their own. We'll wash the stain off our hands, rinsing it down the sink, sip cabernet sauvignon, and discuss our lives and our loves.

The sun sets with a chilly presentation of color as we climb back into the pickup. The wind will howl tonight.

———————

I keep stashing paintings in the nightstand drawer. I keep smearing the sharp primary colors of my emotions over the land until they are more muted, more palatable. I keep seeking to become part of the scene, a part of the action, the interaction, the intimacy. I keep encountering snakes and picking up stones, drawing back my pen and aiming for the heart and the head of the matter.

A Legacy of Snakes and Stones

Small White Squares

My bare toes left the painted concrete steps. I held my chin high and dog-paddled across the still water to my father. He caught me in one arm, his other hand holding a white handkerchief folded into a square. He bowed his head in prayer.

Earlier that day his face reddened as he pounded the pulpit, preaching overtime, emotions spilling down into a congregation surreptitiously glancing at their watches. They wanted to go home to their lives of farming and Sunday afternoon rest; he wanted to fill them with the same passion that kept him locked in a private, inner war. I didn't understand the message, but my mother's silence while she did the dishes in the stillness that followed Sunday dinner drove me out of the parsonage and across to the concrete steps of the country church. I knocked on the door of his office and asked to join his world so he wouldn't be so alone. I was six years old.

After he said amen, he placed the soft handkerchief over my face and laid me under the water.

———•—•———

We left home on Friday morning, skipping school with our parents' blessings, suitcases packed and pillows in our arms. The boys scrambled to the back of the van while the girls sat closer to the adults up front, but turned around often. We sang in the van. We sang in our cabins. We sang fast songs with clapping. We sang slow, pretty songs with harmony.

We had been groomed our whole lives for personal acceptance of a savior and a clan. By the Saturday night meeting, our emotions were on edge from our immersion in the fervent atmosphere and the insistence of every adult that our presence in that place meant we were different, special, set apart. I bowed my head low among the voices lifted in prayer. I wondered if baptism at six still counted at sixteen.

Across the way, a boy with hair that fell over his eyes leaned forward, elbows on his knees, head bowed. His eyes flashed my way, and we smiled where no one could see. I had watched him play volleyball during recreation time that afternoon. Now he was watching me.

Late Sunday evening we stand and sing our new songs for the parents and elders. They ask us who walked down the aisle, who got baptized, and who gave a testimony. Silently I finger the corners of the folded square of notebook paper tucked in my pocket, a note from the boy with hair that fell over his eyes.

———•—————

The concrete steps of my front stoop were warm and rough under my bare feet as I greeted the redheaded preacher making house calls. The toddler was heavy on my hip. My husband and I had recently moved to the area known as Saint's Roost. We had picked which church to attend by counting the number of ranch trucks in the parking lot on a Sunday morning. The preacher was even a former JA cowboy. Now, instead of keeping tallies of cows in the pastures, he was marking down the tallies he would take to the convention of his denomination—chalk up two more strays with calves at side to be added to his count, branded with his iron.

As he pulled a sharp-cornered white note card out of his pocket, he explained that in order to belong to his church we had to be baptized in their baptistery.

"If we choose not to, may we still attend services on Sunday mornings?"

He shifted his weight and lowered the membership card to his side. "Well, yes, of course. But at some point you are going to want to join, to become a member."

"Why?"

"Every Christian needs a church home."

"Why?"

"So that when you die you will have someone to preach your funeral."

———•—•———

The wine was red, glinting in the glasses; the music, real and fresh. The menu listed tapas and tortilla wraps drenched in molé. I ate lox and capers; fresh red strawberries; cheeses I could not name. Outside the snow fell softly on shining black pavement while ideas of art and philosophy kept us warm. In the pooling light, they spoke of living a life of art, of poets, of doing figure studies on Wednesday evenings.

The group was a good mixture of students and teachers, sometimes the lines all blurred. My sister sat across from me at the round tiled table, conversing easily about her master's degree studies in English and literature and philosophies she puts in neat, nice, labeled boxes. A young man I had only known as a cowboy poet talked of folk music and Dylan. A girl wearing a crocheted stocking cap spoke enthusiastically of changing her major. The man beside me was writing a monograph on the creative process.

I was just a ranch wife and mom who had set her writing aside months ago. I didn't know the names of the philosophers they spoke of. I had never heard of the poets. Their hands flew in illustration of their passion, their faces lit from within, and I chose immersion in that new gospel.

He drew on a napkin, a diagram in black ink, a list of books, a progression from Creator to creator along a line that made more sense to me than anything I had ever seen. I was loath to leave that place, those people who lived a life of art and preached it so well. I tucked the white napkin with its lines and lists into my pocket.

———•—•———

There isn't a square in sight, and the night is enormous. Only the moon is white where it bounces off of my clothing lying on the grassy bank, socks, panties, and bra on top of the pile. The moonlight changes to silver when it touches the tops of the trees lining the creek bank or shines on the wet stones at my feet. It turns the pool under the overhanging rock to black ink. The creek chatters into the pool on one side and rushes quickly out on the other after having paused in the slow motion of the swimming hole.

A breeze brings chill bumps to my bare skin and makes the cottonwoods gossip, but it would be silly to get dressed now.

The rocks are smoothly imperfect under my bare feet until they give way to a deep leaf-harboring mud that floats upwards with each step I take. The water inches past my waist, and I lift my feet to swim out into the middle. Now that I've left the shore, the water seems warmer than the air. I open my legs and spread my arms wide and duck beneath its surface to do a clumsy ballet that gets more graceful with each twist. I rise to the surface, open-mouthed and laughing. And here in the blank white moonlight, I duck my head and tuck my knees and do somersaults in the living water.

Rightful Place

"There is so much less pressure, making out with a woman rather than a man." I am lying on a wooden floor beside a twenty-something girl with the soul of a wise old woman, throw pillows under our heads. Her legs are drawn up in an arch, illuminated by the almost full moon shining through the window, her skin the color of the bluestem in the fall.

"There is so much less focus on penetration and climax." She speaks as if offering me a better cleanser for my kitchen sink or a hint on where to buy the perfect dress.

I knew her first from a distance. I admired her swinging walk, her laugh, the unfettered style of her art. I knew her first as the friend of a friend and a girl who all of the guys wanted to meet. She's so young. In some ways untouched by men, she still shows their marks on her soul, their presence in her past dictating her present. She wears strange hats and dinosaur T-shirts with her eyelet skirts. She tells me that she is not girly, but her toenails are painted black and wink with glued-on jewels. Because of her, I am more aware of everyone around me. There is nothing tentative about her affection, and she greets me enthusiastically, even lovingly, and stands with her smooth, freckled arm around my waist, relaxed and committed to holding onto me. She asks me to keep her secrets. I hang around just to hear what she is going to say next. I know her and then I don't.

I lay in bed alone that night, the room darker than before, and smiled as I thought of her words, her youth, the opportunity to embrace another way of thinking, a new idea. The moon had moved away from the windows, up to a place where it threw its light more broadly over the land. Up to a place where it revealed the curves and crevasses of the unplowed prairie. Up to a place where it gave the nightlife that hunted and stirred while the humans slept a rare place to play. I lay there that night and craved the next time I would put my head on the breast of the land, dig my hands into her soil, watch the rain sweep her clean, hear the wind sing along her draws.

I thought about the morrow when I would return to the ranch after a few days away for a workshop, good company, food I didn't prepare myself. Tomorrow would take me back to chores, to kids, to horses, to my husband. Tomorrow would take me back to the land.

———————

Many tomorrows later I stood on the highway side of the cattle guard and looked back over the prairie, the cold biting wind belying spring. That winter we had one blizzard right after the other, overlapping sometimes, always layering new snow over the top of frozen mud.

The mud stayed with us, as did the cold wind.

Spring brought more change and less change than we had expected. Under circumstances that seemed unfair and difficult at the time, we were told that we must leave the Holt Brothers Ranch and were given thirty days to do so. We had been there five years, the longest I had ever lived anywhere in my life. The wind stayed all through March and April as we sold our horses, gave away our dogs, packed, planned, and positioned ourselves for new roads. It blew and blew, both driving us indoors and driving us away.

As I stood there looking back over that piece of land that was never mine but felt so much like home, I realized that, like a first lover, the prairie had prepared me for other terrain, other loves, gave me courage to seek intimacy with other places. During the years we lived on the watershed of the Salt Fork of the Red River I learned to observe with the eyes and heart of an artist. With that backwards look, I was also looking forward. I was taking with me the prairie's lessons of weathering, wondering, and wandering. I took an appreciation of the prairie to every new place I went after we turned onto the highway, headed west.

<hr />

I knew the prairie first from the highways. I admired its curves, river breaks, and shadowy distances seen through vehicle windows when I would drive north up over the caprock. I knew the prairie's rolling vistas that frighten people who prefer to be sheltered from the sky by trees or mountains or buildings. I knew the prairie from books, from poems, from songs about the wind. I knew its small towns with their grain elevators and cotton gins and reduced-speed-ahead signs.

I knew the prairie first by formal names, the Llano Estacado or the Great Plains. I thought it barren and inhospitable. I thought it flat and sexless. I knew it as a cotton field, a wheat field, a tractor enveloped in a cloud of red dirt that spawns dust devils behind. I turned away and shielded my face from the pain of plowed topsoil blowing from county to county. I knew this region by the names of the ranches with their pipe entrances and deeded grasslands.

Five years ago, we moved to this ranch, an almost pristine piece of prairie and river breaks bounded by farmland, an interstate highway, farm-to-market roads, and ranch land owned by other people. Initially I knew this land as a work associate, a terrain to be politely dealt with while the whole family restructured their lives after moving up out of the Palo Duro Canyon. I came to know it by the numbers, the sections, the thermometer, the cattle its grasses can sustain, the location of its windmills, by the boundaries erected by men.

I thought at first that I would not like the flat topography, only to find that

I was perched on a windswept mountain with canyons to the south and the cut banks that feed the Salt Fork of the Red River to the north. The terrain rolls and swells and drops off sharply in places. I thought I would hate the winters up on the divide, only to discover electricity in the air when a blue norther is hovering and about to pounce. I thought the plains were dry, only to discover that water is restless on the prairie, running ever downward until it reaches the low places, furred and dark. After the waters traverse the creases, sometimes rushing, sometimes trickling, sometimes seeping, the prairie cradles the moisture in hollows. Even as it lies shining under the sun, it refuses to rest, always soaking, nurturing, and evaporating . . . duck-rich and frog-perfect. Heel-fly ponds and playa lakes beckon me over, and catch my feet in cow-trodden margins, smearing me with dampness and hope. When the rain refuses to fall, and the pools in the basins have evaporated or sunk or been drunk by cows and deer and dragonflies, when the swallow has carried away the last of the rich mud, the prairie sits burning, giving away moisture from its millions of bladed leaves until they crisp. And still, beneath those crusty layers of grasses, soils, and sands, we float on a freshwater ocean.

This piece of ancient prairie is unplowed by men but still shows their marks, bound by their fences, striated by their roads, and penetrated and pumped in their search for water. Where their cattle don't graze, it is always at risk of being raped for its hardpan caliche or tattooed by a plow's needle teeth to make long red rows for planting. A true painting would blot out the airplane in the clouds, the ribbon of highway to the east, the grain elevators and the radio towers that mar the skyline. It is uncluttered by oil wells, tank batteries, or hunters in the fall, but the mesquites have begun to creep up over the rim of the caprock and the ranch roads snake from windmill to windmill. I mourn my inability to walk over every rise and fall of the land, surprising coyote pups at play, flushing quail and meadowlarks, and watching the seeds travel from place to place. Now that I have come to know this land, this small piece of the Llano Estacado, I am acutely aware of an antelope buck staring at me from behind the sage. I notice every track in the dust and the seasons within the seasons. I dig deeper into the books and poems and songs, until I abandon those written by men and go out to sleep on the prairie instead, laying aside my clocks, my walls, my preconceptions.

I am not the only person who admires this land, but I am the one who is here, being touched by it, with cricket song all around me. I lie on the prairie with a sheet of canvas separating me from the tight grass flat. As the colors I know hide in monochrome moonlight, I trust that I will be safe, without brick or glass or heavy wooden door.

I cannot be tentative when I go to camp on the watershed above the Salt Fork. I must be willing to sweat as I hammer in the tipi stakes and dig in the rocky ridge to make a fire pit. I must be willing to commit to making dead bear grass and cow chips burn. I must tend the coals lest the winds fan them out of control. I must respect every blade, every insect, every thorn, every stone. The moonlight is my reward for enduring buffeting winds and mid-day sun. I will learn to smell the blizzard coming and turn to face the storms. I will hang around to watch the dried grasses crack under a sheet of ice or turn to tinder under a white sun, and never presume to know this land.

The seed doesn't choose where it falls. The seeds of prairie grasses with barbs or corkscrews cling, passengers of foot pad, pelt, or pant leg, fostered or flung afar by feather, fur, or flood.

But a human being must live one step at a time, looking out windows and going through doors. I came to this place, my rightful place, through choice, decision, and progression.

———•———

The prairie doesn't care if I stay or if I go. Every thirty days, with or without me, the full moon rises.

Language of Place, Language of Work

The land and its features inform the language of the people who watch the seasons and walk in its mud. On the Great Plains, when a storm moves in from the north, beginning as a blue line but coming on as strong as a dark black freight train, we call it a **blue norther,** and whether it brings rain or snow, we hope it fills the **playa lakes,** that wonderful prairie phenomenon of shallow, wind-dished catchments that are often only obvious when sufficient moisture has fallen. Playas are naturally occurring seasonal wetlands, historically significant to the Llano Estacado, often overlooked and misunderstood as a resource in the region. To read more about playa lakes, see *Playas: Jewels of the Plains,* by Jim Steiert and Wyman Meinzer.

I refer to **caliche** many times within this book. Caliche is a mineable white hardpan of calcium carbonate that is often used on roadbeds and building sites.

Water is a precious commodity in the Southwest. Windmills are the beautiful flags that mark where the animals, both domestic and wild, come to drink. The **check** is the one-way valve that lets water into but not out of the column pipe at the bottom of a well, and the **leathers** keep the water from leaking back down around the check valve as the mill raises and lowers it to bring that water to the surface. A **sucker rod** connects the fan and the motor to those workings deep inside the well. Nick used metal sucker rods to build the round pen, and old wooden sucker rods make great medieval weapons.

The water goes from the windmill into whatever storage is available via the **lead pipe.** The overflow from the storage at the windmill is often contained in a small pond called a **heel-fly pond,** so named because the cattle stand in the shallow, muddy water to escape pesky heel flies. Another feature beside a windmill is often a **dirt tank** dam to store additional water.

While the language of the cowboy culture—and even the pronunciation of its words—changes from region to region, on most ranches the cowboys speak of **works,** referring to the seasons of the year when the ranch is very busy with crews of men branding calves (spring) or weaning and shipping (fall). Works stands apart from the rest of the year when a **camp man,** a cowboy living on an outlying part of the ranch (a camp), spends his time riding or **prowling** through the cattle, checking his fences and waters, and making sure that after a storm there are no water gaps down. **Water gaps** are the sections of the fence that go across creeks, draws, and watersheds, built to swing or break away instead of letting the water and debris carry the whole fence down the country. Most camp men carry **tally books** in their pockets in which to make tally marks to keep track of how many cattle are in each pasture.

The cowboy may work on a **yearling** outfit, one that fattens cattle before sending them to feedlots, or a cow/calf operation that runs mainly mama cows whose job it is to have a calf each year. On a yearling operation a cowboy in wintertime must worry about **bloat** if he is fattening steers on winter wheat that, when it freezes, can poison the steers, causing them to produce too much gas in the rumen. On a yearling operation, a cowboy must also **process** each load of cattle trucked in, running them through the chute for vaccination and branding. Yearlings often get ill with respiratory diseases contracted during the stress of weaning and/or shipping. Those who never recover but don't die are said to be **chronic.** Cows and yearlings are often fed **cake,** pelleted feed that comes in sacks or bulk. When the animals get used to coming to the feed pickup, it is often called the **suke** (sook) wagon, and it can be used to help move the cattle more easily by luring them with the promise of food. Ranchers often feed vitamins and minerals to cattle by distributing **mineral block** in the pastures.

A cowboy's main tool is the horse, and in the Southwest the group of horses available for use on the ranch is referred to using the Spanish word **remuda.** A **bronc** is a young, not completely trained horse, liable to buck or **pitch.** The **button** is usually the youngest man on the crew, and everyone prefers that the buttons ride the broncs. A **round pen** is a useful place for training young horses. On most large ranches, a cowboy rides horses owned by the ranch, **company horses.** A personal horse is one owned by the cowboy himself.

Cowboy gear varies from region to region. In the Texas panhandle, as in other regions, cowboys trade gear and tack back and forth, and they sometimes refer to the things they have "for trade" as **plunder. Kack** refers to a cowboy's saddle. **Latigos** are the leather straps that hold the saddle's cinches or girths in place. **Oxbows** are a type of stirrup shaped like the bow around an oxen's neck. **Gal-legs** are spurs whose shanks are shaped like a woman's leg. The **hondo** is the small loop in the end of a rope that the rope passes through to create the bigger loop that hopefully will be thrown around the neck or legs of the animal one wishes to catch. Many cowboys own a canvas range **tipi** for sleeping at the wagon. A **brush jacket** is a coat made of heavy canvas that is often worn in summer and winter both. **Leggings,** chaps made of leather, are also necessary where mesquite, cedar, cactus, and oak thickets abound. A short, knee-length pair of chaps are called **chinks.** A **wild rag** is a neck scarf, most of the time worn for warmth, but often worn for adornment as well.

A **piggin' string** is a short length of rope that a cowboy carries on his saddle or on his leggings. Often he has several tied to the headache rack of his pickup and on every trailer gate. He uses these piggin' strings to hobble his horse, tie down animals, tie up gates and fences, and secure errant dogs and children. I used to thread one through the back belt loop on Oscar's size 2T Wranglers to keep him from escaping.

A **cattle pot** is a semitruck designed for hauling livestock. The **crow's nest** is the announcer's stand or judge's box at a rodeo arena. A **dually** is a pickup with dual back wheels. A **gooseneck** is a long horse trailer pulled by a fifth-wheel hitch. A **hot wire** is an electric fence. A **maverick** is a bovine creature that has eluded the cowboys for at least one season and is not branded or earmarked.

When a cowboy on horseback catches something in his rope, he can secure his rope in two ways. He can either **dally** by wrapping the tail of his rope around the saddle horn, or he can be **tied hard and fast** to the saddle horn already via a loop (horn knot) in the tail end of his rope. Team ropers dally in the arena. Many cowboys choose to dally in the branding pen for safety's sake due to close confines. Cowboys in brush country often tie hard and fast, while buckaroos in the northern states feel strongly about dallying. Sermons and poems have been written espousing the merits of each method. Many men have lost fingers to dallying. Most stories about big wrecks start out with, "I was tied off, see, and went to rope this old cow." When I first introduced Nick to my paternal grandfather, Papa pressed his five-foot, five-inch frame up close to Nick's six-foot, five-inch frame and asked, "Son, do you dally or tie hard and fast?"

Cowboys use the phrase to **sull up** when an animal or human becomes sullen and refuses to cooperate. A cow that is hot and mad will sull up and hide in the brush. A young horse that is frustrated by his lessons will sull up and quit. Ranch wives sull up, cross their arms, and raise their eyebrows for a variety of reasons.

About the Author

Amy Hale Auker writes essays, poems, and fiction while working for day wages on an Arizona ranch. Twenty years on commercial cattle operations in Texas—cooking for cowboys, homeschooling children, and taking long walks—have given her material for writing about a way of life that is alive and well in the heart of the American West. She lives in Prescott, Arizona.